BEYOND GENDER:

THE NEW RULES OF LEADERSHIP

WRITTEN BY

RÚNA MAGNÚSDÓTTIR

What do people say about this book?

"Beyond Gender: The New Rules of Leadership offers a riveting departure from conventional leadership paradigms, steering us towards a future where leadership is defined by vision and diversity, not gender. With her exceptional insight, Rúna challenges leaders to break free from the gender matrix that has long dictated norms and to lead with authenticity and inclusivity. Each of the 20 chapters serve as stepping stones to redefining leadership success, blending vulnerability, humor, and practical wisdom. This book is more than a guide; it's an invitation to transform how we lead and empower others in an AI-enhanced world. *Beyond Gender* is an indispensable read for anyone ready to forge a path of impactful leadership in today's dynamic global landscape."

~ **Dr. Marshall Goldsmith** is the *Thinkers50* #1 Executive Coach and New York Times bestselling author of *The Earned Life, Triggers,* and *What Got You Here Won't Get You There.*

You're in for a treat.

Runa has a great and wise mind and a gift for capturing the thoughts of other great minds. In her inimitable style, she then adds a few left-field ideas and relays it all back in an engaging, thought-provoking, and entertaining way. Transition times are troubling for societies and us as individuals. As we traverse our evolutionary jump from box-based binary thinking to allowing many possibilities of being to exist simultaneously, we need leaders like Runa to show us the way.

~ **Nicholas Haines,** co-founder of No More Boxes

Transformational Movement

This is a book about freedom and utilising humanity's full potential. *Freedom for the individual. Freedom for society. Free from any limiting individual and societal construct. For each of us to contribute with our unique contribution, that is what we need. How else can we be 100 percent inner guided and find our soul work? Humanity is taking a quantum leap these years. We are reinventing ourselves and our organisations. This book will help propel us in this new direction. Thinking outside of the box. Listen, the future is calling for this.*

~ Susanne Frandsen, International Author, Speaker, and Executive Coach

If you read any book this year, make this book a priority. You will be so glad you did.

Everyone asks: What can I do? Begin with putting into practice the recommendations from this book. Runa's wisdom, insights, and executive experience will touch your heart and change your mind if you are a wise leader. This book is mandatory reading for all executive decision-makers, business leaders, and teams. Be a part of changing this world of work and do your part to make yourself count in history.

~ Dr. David Paul, author, academic, and executive advisor

Rúna Magnúsdóttir's life journey has consistently defied convention, and her book will ignite the spark within you to do the same. If you're a leader, whether in life or your career, this perspective is a treasure trove waiting to be uncovered. Exploring it could be the key to elevating yourself and those you lead to a realm of genuine authenticity, which lies at the heart of meaningful engagement.

~ Wendy Watkins, a professional, compassionate human being

FOREWORD

I will keep this short because you have something important to do. Read this book.

Beyond Gender: The New Rules of Leadership is a guide to an exciting and, at times, confusing evolutionary leap that humans are trying to attempt.

To move into the Quantum field.

The best way to get your head around that pathetic attempt to sound deep and mysterious is to appreciate the differences between a regular and a quantum computer.

Regular computers are the equivalent of reading a book one page at a time. It's slow and laborious, and however fast you can read, there is a limit to how much you can get through. Quantum computers, on the other hand, are magical. They can read every page simultaneously while reading another ten books in the same way at the same time.

As a result, a regular computer will take 47 years to do what a quantum computer can do in less than 6 seconds. Currently, most humans are like traditional computers.

We tend to see things in a binary, boxed-based way. And for good reason. In the early days of our evolution, we had to work out what was safe and what was a threat. And save our brain calories. So, we made generalisations about people and things.

Men are like this. Women are like that. And so on. We did it with everything and everyone and created roles and responsibilities that matched our box-based perception. Books were written, stories were told, rules were made, and it became our truth.

Rúna, in her magnificent, warm and incredible style with

Beyond Gender: The New Rules of Leadership, will show you what it's like if we saw beyond boxes and genders. Imagine how our workplace and the world would be if we could do the equivalent of witnessing every dimension of a person at once and all their possible versions. And at the same time, they and we could exist in all situations.

That is going quantum and the next stage of human evolution.

Now, head off and read this book. Rúna will guide you through the first stages as the Icelandic genius she is.

Sorry, Rúna, I just put you in two boxes.

November 2023

Nick xx

Contents

BEYOND

GENDER

INTRODUCTION

Welcome to a world where the boundaries imposed by gender norms and expectations dissolve, where leadership extends beyond predefined roles, and where your unique qualities and strengths are celebrated without the confines of societal scripts.

Imagine a realm where you dare to shine your brightest, and in return, you witness the brilliance of those around you— your team, your colleagues, your family—all embracing their fullest potential.

Step into the domain of *Beyond Gender: The New Rules of Leadership!*—a journey that transcends the ordinary and propels us towards an extraordinary leadership paradigm. A paradigm where you see and value yourself and others for who you are, not by the script or the box that society has placed you in by your gender.

This is more than just a book; it's a dynamic expedition fuelled by years of dedication to gender equity. As a former vice president for FKA, the Association of Women Business Leaders in Iceland, and the founder of one of the first online communities for women entrepreneurs, Connected Women, I've passionately championed the cause of gender equality. I've been internationally recognised and awarded by prestigious organisations like the Women's Economic Forum (WEF) and Women Innovators Inventors Network (WIIN) for my work. I've spoken at several international and national conferences and events to empower women to improve their game.

My commitment is further reflected in my role on countless advisory boards to bring greater gender equality.

Why I'm Passionate About This

Let me share a bit about myself and why this book holds a special place in my heart.

As mentioned above, I hail from Iceland, a country that has shown the world the transformative power of unity and determination to reach gender equality. I was there in October 1975, when women of all ages marched through the streets, demanding recognition for their contributions. Witnessing this event and being there myself, not to mention seeing my mother and her girlfriends march downtown to demonstrate they were just as essential to the economy as men were, ignited a fire in me—the fire to drive change and shatter the glass ceiling that still lingers.

In 1980, I witnessed President Vigdis Finnbogadottir become the first democratically elected female president.

Wow . . . that was something. Before the election, I remember Ms. Vigdis's brilliance when a TV reporter asked her in an interview, "Now, you've gone through cancer treatment and have had one of your breasts removed. How are you going to lead a nation with only one breast?" Vigdis's reply was spot-on when she said candidly, "Well, I'm not going to breastfeed the nation!" And hey, she won the election!

Even though I grew up in a family that fostered individuality and lively conversations, I often questioned why my brother was trusted with odd things, such as using the family car without a special caution talk beforehand or getting certain freedoms simply because he was a boy, when the same didn't hold true for me. The distinction was baffling. Why were my abilities curtailed based on my gender? It wasn't just in my family; societal expectations echoed the same sentiment. I vividly recall my parents emphasising the importance of being diplomatic rather than straightforward, assuming that women should navigate situations more delicately. This journey led me to question the origins of such perspectives and fuelled my determination to break free from these limitations.

Despite our progress, gender equality is not fully realised, even in places like Iceland. Numbers and reports tell us one story, but lived experiences tell another. As a leadership coach with years of experience and through thousands of coaching sessions, I've witnessed the incredible potential humans possess when they step into their true power.

I know change is possible because I've seen it happen—in individuals, communities, and even nationally.

At the same time, I'm aware as human beings, we are creatures of habits.

The economic crash of 2008 in Iceland was like a plot twist in a thrilling novel, propelling women into leadership positions in ways no one could have predicted.

As the old norms crumbled like a poorly baked pastry, a new narrative emerged: women were suddenly hailed as icons and saviours, the chosen ones to lead us out of the financial abyss. It was like they had a secret leadership manual that men had misplaced. People started to believe that women possessed magical listening powers, an innate risk radar, and a PhD in work–life balance. In short, they were seen as masters of collaboration with egos the size of a teardrop.

Essentially, folks began to believe that women would swoop in and save the country, maybe even the world. While this shift undeniably brought more women into leadership roles and ushered in positive changes, it posed its fair share of complex challenges.

Now, let's rewind a bit. I've been championing women's empowerment for decades, but something about the narrative needed to still didn't add up for me.

The more women climbed the ladder, the wider the chasm seemed to grow between the genders. It felt like we were stuck in this never-ending conversation where women were portrayed as goddesses and men as inherently toxic.

Frankly, I didn't buy into either extreme. And at the same time, I felt stuck.

That moment, speaking at the United Nations Global Summit, changed everything.

But my "aha" moment came in March 2018 at the Impact Leadership 21 Global Summit at the United Nations Headquarters in New York City. I was there with a few of my changemakers to discuss gender equality, peace, and sustainability—pretty weighty. That's when my business partner, Nick Haines, dropped a truth bomb. He explained why we were struggling to achieve our sustainable development goals: "It's because we keep putting people into boxes," he said, adding, "While categorisation helps us understand the world's complexity, the problem arises when we expect individuals to live and behave solely within these boxes."

It felt like the universe had hit me with a cosmic wake-up call at that moment. It became clear that fighting for women's rights wasn't the silver bullet for gender equality. We needed to strive for gender *equity*. This wasn't only about empowering women, regardless of who they were, where they were coming from, or what they wanted in life. We also needed to liberate men from society's constraints, who were trying hard to fulfil the role society had placed on them, believing they had it all just because they were men. It was about dismantling the walls that caged everyone, regardless of gender.

This revelation sparked a tectonic shift in my perspective. It was no longer about elevating one gender at the expense of the other. It was about breaking down the barriers that held us from realising our full potential, free from societal expectations.

With this newfound clarity, my mission evolved into a holistic transformation of leadership that empowers everyone to break free from limitations and become authentic leaders in their own right.

Only then could we see who we are, not the script we've been following, and we could value our unique selves and those around us. We could guide ourselves and others to a better world with a new script that enables us to be true to ourselves.

It was time to rewrite the leadership playbook, and this book is the first draft of that exciting journey.

Finding the Courage to Write

But I needed the courage to pen my journey and transformative insight.

I started the book four times and never got further than chapter 3 or 4.

The magnitude of the responsibility weighed on me. Doubts and questions swirled in my mind. Could I truly make a difference? Was I equipped to articulate such a profound shift in leadership paradigms?

I put the project aside, not knowing if I would ever have the courage to write and share my thoughts and insights.

The birth of my granddaughter gave me the courage to continue.

It wasn't until I looked into the eyes of my newborn granddaughter, Helena Bryndís, in February 2023, that the answer became resoundingly clear. Her innocence and boundless potential became a mirror reflecting my purpose. I realised that by undertaking this endeavour, I could help shape a world where she would grow up free from the confines that held generations before her. And even if nobody else would read the book, at least perhaps one day, she could read it herself and think: "Ahh . . . this is what my grandma was passionate about."

Rewriting the Rules

Here, you'll discover a road map to redefine leadership and rewrite the rules that have held us back for too long. Are you ready to seize the reins of your journey, navigate uncharted territories, and chart a course towards personal and collective transformation?

Are you prepared to challenge the status quo and explore an entirely new dimension of leadership that transcends gender biases?

Why This Book Matters

Before diving into this book's heart, let me clarify my purpose. This is about more than just leadership; it's about leadership that enables you to guide yourself and others into a future where gender biases are dismantled. It's about a world where we are free to be ourselves. A world where we value people for who they are.

But what exactly do we mean by "Beyond Gender: The New Rules of Leadership"?

Picture a world where gender roles and potential precede societal norms and do not restrict leadership. This is a world where the true essence of leadership is not confined by expectations or assumptions based on the box we put people in by their gender, race, religion, or background. Instead, it is unleashed through an individual's strengths, passion, values, unique skills, experiences, knowledge, and capabilities.

Picture yourself feeling safe and free, able to be yourself as the person you were born to be and having the confidence and the tools to guide yourself and others to a better world.

As a reader of this book, you hold in your hands more than just pages bound together; you have the key to unlocking transformative leadership.

Throughout these chapters, you will gain insights and actively engage through powerful exercises to facilitate your growth and self-discovery.

I will share tips, insights, tools, and stories for you to become a leader who leads beyond gender.

What You Can Expect

What can you expect from this book? Each chapter explores a new facet of leadership beyond gender. We'll dive deep into energies, neuroscience, mindfulness, quantum physics, and more to unearth strategies to expand your horizons and create space for your growth.

This journey isn't just about reading but active participation.

Throughout the book, you'll encounter hands-on exercises encouraging reflection, confrontation of biases, and embracing growth opportunities. You'll actively shape your transformation.

You will probably see things differently than the viewpoint I'm sharing, which is okay. I may share something that is quite the opposite of what you believe the world to be.

All I ask of you is to keep an open mind.

Your Call to Action

As we embark on this journey together, I invite you to engage with the content thoroughly, reflect on your experiences, and commit to action.

The pages ahead are not just words; they're a road map to a world where leadership knows no bounds, authenticity is celebrated, and your unique potential becomes your guiding light.

So, are you ready to challenge what you've been told about gender norms? Are you prepared to step into a new dimension of leadership that transcends expectations and creates a brighter future for yourself and those around you?

The adventure awaits. Let's break the chains of gender bias and claim our roles as leaders beyond genders. The stage is set, and the curtain is about to rise. Are you ready to take your place in this transformative journey?

Oops . . . one more thing before we head into chapter 1.

Since you already have this book in your hands or on your electronic device, that tells me you are one step closer to becoming a leader who leads beyond gender. In this book, I will communicate with you as a leader on this transformational journey.

Let's start with the benefit of reading this book and answering the questions for each chapter.

Here are the ten things you will benefit from as a leader who leads beyond gender.

10 Transformations You'll Witness in Your Life:

1. **Unleash Your Authentic Self:** You will say goodbye to conforming to societal norms and embrace your true self unapologetically.

2. **Challenge Gender Scripts:** You can navigate the leadership terrain with a different outlook, even wholly without gender-specific expectations and assumptions.

3. **Expand Leadership Horizons:** You will be able to embrace a holistic understanding of leadership that transcends gender constraints.

4. **Elevate Diversity & Inclusion:** You can cultivate environments where everyone's unique strengths are celebrated.

5. **Foster Authentic Communication:** You can communicate openly and empathetically, fostering mutual understanding, starting at your kitchen table.

6. **Rewrite Leadership Narratives:** You will create new narratives emphasising stability, not stereotypes.

7. **Cultivate Emotional Intelligence:** You will work on and develop emotional intelligence that enables compassionate and effective leadership.

8. **Fuel Empowerment:** You will have access to empower yourself and others to lead without limitations, valuing everyone's individual attributes.

9. **Challenge Biases:** You will be able to recognise and confront unconscious biases, fostering an inclusive leadership approach.

10. **Inspire Collective Change:** You can pave the way for a world where leadership is defined by passion, purpose, and impact.

So, are you prepared to challenge those gender norms? Are you ready to wield your unique qualities and guide others towards an authentic and empowered leadership journey?

If you're ready to embrace the possibilities, this book is your guide. Buckle up, for we're about to embark on a transformative journey to reshape your understanding of leadership. This journey isn't for the faint of heart; it's for those ready to challenge norms, spark conversations, and ignite real change.

It's time to unveil the curtain on "The New Rules of Leadership"—way beyond gender!

Are you up for the challenge?

Let's do this.

Breaking Free from the Gender Matrix: Unlocking the New Rules to Leadership

Are you ready to give the boot to outdated norms and stride into a world where your leadership prowess knows no gender-bound bounds? Well, here's your ticket to rewriting the playbook!

Let's dive into chapter 1, where we're setting the stage for a seismic shift. Think of it as the prelude to a ground-breaking symphony of leadership evolution. We're stepping into the arena of twenty-first-century leadership, a domain where the shackles of gender no longer hold sway.

Get ready for an exhilarating ride that will challenge your perceptions, broaden your horizons, and ignite the flames of transformative change.

But first, picture this: people being seen as who they are. That could mean men rocking dresses with lipstick just as fabulously as women swing trousers, suits, and dresses. Or people of all genders, races, or ages leading businesses, organisations, communities, their countries, or the world.

Leaders beyond genders are the trailblazers of this new era, rewriting the narrative of traditional norms. They acknowledge their biases, confront the 188 societal preconceptions that sneakily creep into our minds, and shatter the gender matrix holding us hostage. More about our biases in chapter 7.

Sound out of the box?

Remember when women in the Western world were frowned upon for wearing trousers and needed special saddles for their horses?

Times have changed, my friend, and those gender lines are about to blur even more.

But hold on. This isn't just a woman's crusade; it's a symphony of human empowerment. It's about unleashing your inner leadership maestro, regardless of the blueprint that genetics handed you. Society has been out of tune for too long, expecting men to be money magicians and women to be caring cultivators.

Well, guess what? The era of that performance is over, and we're rewriting the new melody note by note.

Let's flip the lens and gaze upon the terrain of leadership. Picture a world where leadership isn't a gender-locked treasure chest but a vibrant tapestry woven from the threads of authenticity, resilience, and innovation. The domain of leadership beyond gender isn't just a sunny beach for women; it's a lush forest where both men and women can dance side by side, unburdened by outdated gender constructs.

Why am I so adamant about this shift?

As I mentioned in the introduction, I hail from Iceland, where gender norms were shattered like ice on a warm day. I've seen how emancipation from societal boxes allows people to march to the beat of their own drums. The more we shed the gender-weighted costumes, the more we waltz into a world where leadership creates space for people to thrive, feeling free to share what they bring to the table, not the gender tag they wear.

My journey has taught me that leadership isn't a restricted VIP lounge; it's an all-access pass up for grabs by anyone daring to seize it. Leading my own life became my mantra, steering me through challenges and teaching me that knowing oneself is the compass that guides authentic leadership. It's about tapping into your vitality, harnessing your uniqueness, and letting that light shine like a cosmic disco ball.

Let's call a spade a spade. This gender-blurring symphony might sound like a record scratch in some corners of the world. Challenging societal norms can stir up a storm. Witnessing the resistance is disheartening, but I won't be silenced. I've seen the transformation and am here to share the truth.

Here's the grand reveal: leadership isn't some exclusive gala; it's a block party open to all. It's the DNA of empowerment, the catalyst for change, and the passport to a world where authentic expression reigns supreme. When we embrace leadership beyond gender, we spotlight authenticity, inclusion, and the sheer power of the individual.

It's about leading with heart, wisdom, and a splash of audacity.

So, my friend, as we peel back the layers of this book, brace yourself for revelations, aha moments, and a roller-coaster ride of transformation. We'll break down biases, debunk myths, and navigate the waters of gender-inclusive leadership like fearless explorers. Each chapter is a treasure trove of insights, tools, and stories that will equip you on this epic odyssey.

But why stop at mere insights?

Let's roll up our sleeves and dive into the nitty-gritty of discovering your authentic self. We'll ponder powerful questions, don our detective hats to unmask biases, and explore the magical moments that make your heart sing. Get ready to embrace your inner compass and navigate towards a life where joy, purpose, and authenticity reign supreme.

And here's a sneak peek: we'll unlock the vault of wisdom with conversations I've been having through *The Change Makers Podcast, Leadership Beyond Gender* series with experts in the personal development field, neuroscience, epigenetics, meditations, and mindfulness.

Trust me, the dots they connect will light up your path like a galaxy of possibilities.

So, fasten your seat belt as we journey together, forging a path where leadership defies gender boundaries.

Challenging "Norms"

Let's be clear here! We can challenge norms, ignite conversations, and champion authenticity with every step. Our societies create all of these so-called norms. They are all made up. They are all created in our minds, so redefining them should be possible.

Your unique leadership symphony is waiting to be composed, and it's time to let it echo through the halls of time. Let's break those gender chains and claim the stage as leaders beyond gender, one bold stride at a time.

CHAPTER 2

Peer Pressure from Beyond the Grave: Escaping the Grip of Dead People's Opinions

Imagine being trapped in a gender box governed by the opinions of people long gone. A box that only accepts a tiny fraction of what you have to offer to the world. A box that is airtight and smells like old socks. A box that gives you the illusion that living in it keeps you safe. At the same time, it is holding you back from showing your brilliant light.

Oh, hang on a minute. You don't have to imagine. You are already there!

It's the world as most of us see it!

It's your everyday life!

It's there from the moment you wake up every day. You feel it all around you on social media, at home, at work, and even in your gym.

Take a good look. What has it given you?

Has it given you the freedom to determine your soul's calling? Has it enabled you to find out who you are and your unique gifts and superpowers? Does it empower you daily to thrive as the highest version of yourself?

No, I don't think so.

The Confined Framework of the Gender Box

The gender box is an intangible, yet confining, framework woven into our culture across generations. It's a rigid structure that limits our perception of being a man or a woman. Over time, society has etched distinct roles, behaviours, and aspirations for each gender, leading us to view individuals through a narrow lens.

For instance, traditional male roles might include being the breadwinner, the stoic provider who suppresses emotions to maintain an air of strength. On the other hand, female roles often encompass the caregiver and homemaker and are expected to nurture and prioritise family over personal ambitions.

These boxes have become so deeply embedded that we unwittingly accept them as the only options. This conformity stifles authenticity and hinders diversity. However, the moment we shatter these limitations, an inspiring transformation occurs. By expanding the confines of these gender boxes, we grant ourselves and others the opportunity to blossom beyond societal confines.

The Illusion of Safety

Our boxes are designed to make us feel safe. They are designed to make us trust the familiar. And they are great when they do that. It's just that sometimes, these so-called "safe" boxes are the boxes holding you back from being your highest self. They can seem like a good box, but at the same time, they can be bad and even ugly, hence my book: *The Story of Boxes, The Good, The Bad and The Ugly.*

It's time to break free from the peer pressure of dead people and reclaim our autonomy.

This chapter will expose the ridiculousness of living according to outdated stereotypes. If we want to thrive and allow ourselves and the people around us to succeed, we've got to wake up from that illusion. A bit like what the Barbies did in Barbie Land when they woke up from the spell the patriarchal system had placed on them—yes, I'm referring to *Barbie*, the movie.

We've got to get ready to rise above the noise and embrace a reality where we define who we are, irrespective of the expectations of the departed.

On the path to liberation, let's talk about something that might seem a bit eerie but is oh-so-real: *peer pressure from beyond the grave.*

Yes, you heard that right. As if the stress from our living, breathing friends and family wasn't enough, now we're dealing with opinions from people who have long taken the exit ramp from this crazy carnival called life.

In our journey of breaking free from the peer pressure of dead people's opinions, we must recognise that, as human beings, we're wired to repeat patterns. Our brains seek the familiar and comfortable, often leading us down the well-trodden paths our ancestors once walked.

Certain things might feel safe or proper to do because "everyone" around you has done them for generations.

And I'm sure some traditions are very well meant, but are they holding on to the stereotypical gender roles, or are they giving you, your friends, and your family the freedom to live your best life? Ask yourself regularly, how can I become better, bolder, and brighter as the leading light in my life?

In a messed-up world, we need more leaders who transcend the limitations of gender roles and profoundly understand the value of self-awareness. They grasp the significance of peeling away the layers of tradition, habits, and rituals, recognising them for what they are—only fragments of the truth, not the entirety of it. These leaders pave the way for a brighter, more inclusive future by seeing beyond the surface and embracing their authenticity. They're the navigators who chart new courses, honouring the past while forging ahead, acknowledging that actual progress requires understanding the complexities of our human nature.

Let's face it: we're all trapped in this cosmic gender box, but the box walls were built by people who shuffled off from this mortal coil ages ago.

They left their opinions behind, and like stubborn ghosts, these opinions are haunting us, dictating our choices, and chaining us to outdated stereotypes.

But guess what? We can exorcise those ghostly opinions and break free from their spectral grip.

Let's unveil four points that expose just how ridiculous it is to keep living our lives according to the echoes of the past:

1. **Fashion Police from the Afterlife**: Can you believe that we're still dressing up or down based on the notions of people who didn't have access to electric toothbrushes, let alone Instagram? They might have been geniuses in their time, but let's face it: Why isn't it all right for men to wear skirts, dresses, or trousers without being called out? Women can make the choice. Why not men?

2. **Career Clues from the Ancients**: Let me get this straight. We're allowing the opinions of people who thought the earth was flat to shape our career choices. Yes, we're letting their whispers from beyond tell us what we should or shouldn't do for a living. They wouldn't even recognise a smartphone, let alone understand our cutting-edge jobs. What is the purpose of keeping genders in particular job roles? To keep them in place, holding us hostage just because once upon a time, things were this way and not the other.

3. **Relationship Advice from Yesteryears**: Oh, the good ol' days when a dozen roses and a dramatic serenade were the way to win someone's heart. But let's be honest: our hearts don't exactly flutter at seeing someone scaling our balcony like Romeo. Times have changed, and so have our love stories. It's time to update the romance manual. Leaders who lead beyond genders will create space for themselves and others to love whom they want to love!

4. **No More Cookie-Cutter Dreams**: Our long-gone advisors had a thing for cookie-cutter dreams. Back then, there were roles and expectations, and you better fit into them like a perfectly shaped puzzle piece. But news flash: people desire freedom. We no longer live in a time of sepia-toned rigidity. We're living in an era where we've been told we can be anything—CEOs, dancers, astronauts, and poets, all in the same breath—so it's time we create space for people to become what they desire.

Now, let's talk about the perks of being a leader beyond genders, someone who's ready to rise above the noise and embrace a reality where you define who you are, irrespective of the opinions of the dearly departed.

Three things you will see more of in your life as a leader who leads beyond genders:

1. **The Joy of Authenticity**: When you leave the shadows of outdated expectations, you're stepping into a world where your authenticity shines like a beacon. The freedom to know and be yourself is an unmatched joy. And you know the best part? No ghostly critique can dim your glow.

2. **Inspiring the Future**: When you gently challenge the norms of yesterday, you're making way for a brighter tomorrow. You are creating that crack when the earth opens up, and a volcano erupts. The trailblazing you do today could set the stage for a generation that refuses to be shackled by the past. You're not just rewriting your story but creating a narrative for others.

3. **Harnessing Your Inner Maverick**: Leaders beyond genders aren't bound by the chains of tradition. They're the mavericks who harness the power of progress and channel it into innovation. Your forward-thinking mindset becomes the driving force that propels industries, relationships, and the world itself.

As you venture into the wilds of change, remember that the ghosts of yesteryears might have left their opinions behind. At the same time, as we embark on our journey to liberate ourselves from the lingering influence of past generations, it's crucial to approach this transformation with compassion and understanding.

While we aim to break free from the confinements of outdated norms, let's remember that our ancestors did their best in the context of their times. Instead of denigrating the earlier versions of how things used to be, let's express gratitude for their efforts and acknowledge our progress.

Simultaneously, let's stand firm in our resolve to craft a future aligned with our ideals. Leaders beyond gender understand the delicate balance between honouring the past and nurturing a vision for a world that reflects the change they wish to see. In doing so, they become the architects of a reality where gender knows no bounds and authenticity takes centre stage.

It's always up to us to choose whether to let those whispers of old guide us or to rise above them and be the leaders who transcend the limitations of time.

CHAPTER 3

Embracing Our Superpowers: Unleashing the Leader Within

Within each of us lies the potential for remarkable leadership. It's not about fitting into moulds but embracing and unleashing our unique superpowers.

In this chapter, we'll explore the essence of our superpowers and learn how to embed them for extraordinary leadership. Are you ready to tap into your unique strengths, embrace your quirks, and become the superhero leader you were always meant to be?

Unlocking the doors to exceptional leadership starts by tapping into your superpower. It's not about conforming to moulds but embracing the distinct essence that sets you apart. As we journey through this chapter, the spotlight turns to the superpower within you waiting to be utilised.

So, are you ready to dig deep, embrace your quirks, and step into the shoes of the extraordinary leader you're destined to become?

In a world where stereotypes often dictate norms, a refreshing truth emerges. Imagine it as your unique quality, distinguishing you from a crowd of conformity.

In 2012, I embarked on a journey to explore this idea through my book *Branding Your X-Factor*, where I introduced a five-step formula to uncover your X-factor and confidently discover who you authentically are and how to present yourself to the world. Now, we're about to delve even deeper into this concept.

Your X-factor is an intriguing enigma, isn't it? Our super-powers, or X-factors, often remain hidden from our view. Society's constructs have led us to fit into predefined boxes, obscuring the most exceptional aspects of who we are.

I love the analogy presented by Nick Haines, the mastermind behind The Vitality Test and my collaborator in co-founding the No More Boxes Transformational Movement. He likens this to a butterfly that peers at its reflection, seeing only a plump, hairy body. The butterfly fails to recognise the magnificence of its intricate wings. Similarly, we overlook our potential and authenticity while trying to fit into societal moulds.

Perhaps you've grown up in an environment where roles were strictly divided by gender—women as caregivers and men as providers. Or maybe you were taught that self-promotion is wrong or that standing up and speaking out is reserved for certain positions. These societal narratives become ingrained, stifling our genuine expression.

But here's the awakening: you can choose to blaze a new trail and step beyond these confines one step at a time. It's a journey, peeling away layers of conditioning that have accumulated over the years.

I think there is one small word that needs to be repeated here, and that's the word "**can.**"

What emerges is the core of who you are—your superpower. And here's the exciting twist. This journey is about more than just you. It's a paradigm shift. It's about giving people around you space to show up as their authentic selves and shifting your own perspective.

When you embark on this voyage of self-discovery, a profound transformation unfurls. As you uncover your superpower, you redirect your focus away from external opinions.

But remember, this is a journey that requires patience and persistence.

Why is unearthing your superpower a game-changer?

1. **Elevating Self-Leadership:** Grasping your superpower's essence leads to unparalleled self-awareness and direction. It becomes a magnetic force pulling you towards authenticity and infusing your self-leadership with unshakeable conviction.

2. **Guiding Organisations and Groups:** Pushing past gender boundaries isn't only about personal transformation; it's about revolutionising the environments we navigate as leaders. When armed with the knowledge of your superpower, you catalyse change within organisations and groups. Your authenticity ignites a fire, motivating others to uncover their unique strengths and fostering inclusivity and empowerment.

3. **Navigating Global Leadership:** Picture world leaders embracing their superpowers, leading from a place of authenticity rather than ego. When you tap into your superpower, you access wisdom, empathy, and innovation. This trio equips you to navigate the complexities of global leadership with purpose and a transformative vision.

But let's not ignore the flip side. What happens when we remain unaware of our superpowers? When societal expectations obscure our authenticity?

Here are the pitfalls:

1. **Superficial Leadership:** Leading without self-awareness and authenticity is like sailing a ship without a compass. Without depth and resonance, your leadership is shallow and ineffective.

2. **Enforcing Stereotypes:** Not embracing your superpower inadvertently discourages others from exploring their talents. You perpetuate the cycle of conformity.

3. **Diminished Impact:** The world craves leaders who light the path to progress. By shying away from authenticity, you contribute to a world bound by outdated norms, limiting humanity's potential.

As we conclude this chapter, remember this: the potential for remarkable leadership resides within each of us. The journey isn't about fitting in but embracing and unleashing your superpower onto the world stage.

Through exploring our unique strengths, we've learned how to harness these powers for unparalleled leadership.

So, are you ready to tap into your distinctive strengths, confidently embrace your individuality, and rise as the extraordinary leader you were meant to be?

In a world overflowing with stereotypes, the undeniable truth beckons. Your superpower awaits. Think of it as your X-factor, the exceptional quality distinguishing you from the crowd.

But here's the kicker: our superpowers often remain veiled, obscured by the weight of societal expectations. These expectations become our internal scripts, limiting our authentic expression.

But let's awaken.

You can opt for a different narrative, stepping beyond these boundaries one stride at a time. This is a journey, peeling away layers of conditioning that have accumulated over the years.

What emerges is your authentic self—your superpower.

When you embark on this journey, you create a ripple effect of transformation. As you uncover your superpower, you shift the spotlight from external opinions to inner authenticity. It's like igniting a torch within, illuminating the path for others to discover their unique qualities.

So, let's embark on this journey. Peel away conditioning, shed external opinions, and reveal the brilliance of your superpower. Lead beyond gender and boundaries, shaping a world celebrating authenticity and empowering everyone's unique potential.

Reflective Questions for Exploring Your Superpowers

As we conclude this chapter on embracing your superpowers, take a moment to dive deeper into your own journey.

Grab a pen and paper or open a digital note-taking app and embark on an exercise to explore your unique strengths.

1. **Reflect on Passions:** Consider activities that ignite your passion and make you lose track of time. These reveal your talents and interests.

2. **Uncover Uniqueness:** Think about attributes that set you apart. What do people appreciate in you? Write down distinct qualities.

3. **Recall Achievement:** Remember accomplishments that made you proud. What skills or strengths did you tap into? Write them down.

4. **Visualise Ideal Leadership:** Picture yourself as a leader making a significant impact. What qualities do you want to bring? Jot down these attributes.

5. **Identify Your Superpower:** Review your answers for patterns. This could be your superpower—your unique essence.

6. **Set an Intention:** Based on your reflections, commit to integrating your superpower into your journey. Write a statement encapsulating your commitment to authenticity and positive change.

This exercise is just a start. Revisit your reflections whenever you need a reminder of your strengths.

The moment for transformation is now. Your superpower awaits.

CHAPTER 4

The Gender Blender:
Blurring the Lines of Masculinity and Femininity

"Gender doesn't define our energies; our unique blend of energies defines us. Social conditioning may whisper, but it's up to us to compose the melody of our true selves."
—Nick Haines.

Welcome to the most spectacular show in town—the Gender Blender! Get ready for the performance of the century as we send gender stereotypes spinning in a whirlwind.

Buckle up, because we're about to explore the vibrant tapestry of energies that define our humanity.

This chapter shatters the "blue is for boys, and pink is for girls" illusion. Bid farewell to rigid labels and say hello to a realm where energies take centre stage.

Enter the scene, the maestro of energies, the enigmatic Nicholas Haines, fondly known as Nick Haines, my partner in the No More Boxes Transformational Movement.

Nick is a luminary with over thirty-five years of expertise in the Chinese energy field.

A seasoned acupuncturist and visionary, he's peeled back layers of human experience, uncovering the intricate interplay of energies that course through us.

But that's not all. Nick's genius extends beyond healing bodies. He's a trailblazer in unravelling the mysteries of the soul.

His revolutionary creation, The Vitality Test, delves deep into the fabric of one's essence, revealing personality, strengths, and purpose. With a blend of ancient wisdom and modern insight, Nick Haines is your guide to transcending gendered energies and embracing the kaleidoscope of your authentic self.

Let's turn the spotlight on five profound insights emerging from this journey.

According to ancient Chinese wisdom, you made a promise to the world when you were born. This could be a promise to do something, be someone, experience something, learn something, etc.

The universe gave you a blend of five energies: water, wood, fire, earth, and metal energies.

None of these energies is confined by gender; they're about the unique blend of energies within all of us.

The field of energy is a fascinating concept. When you look at it with insights from quantum physics and epigenetics, you see a brilliant pattern that shows you so much of who you are, how you perceive the world, and how others see you.

This is an exciting and breathtaking methodology. I use the Vitality Test myself to help my clients become better, bolder, and brighter.

You can discover your personal chart of vitality by taking the test for yourself here: https://thevitalitytest.com. It's a FREE test!

In this chapter, I will only discuss one part of each energy, meaning the core soul question each energy is subconsciously looking to answer.

Let's examine those five energies and their core soul questions.

1. **Water Energy – The Pursuit of Safety:** Picture water flowing effortlessly, seeking equilibrium. Its core soul question is uncomplicated: "Am I safe? Is this safe?" This transcends gender. It's an innate human desire for security, as Nick Haines reminds us.

2. **Wood Energy – The Yearning for Freedom:** Ah, the essence of wood energy—reaching for the sky without restraint. Its core soul question echoes: "Am I free or trapped?" This isn't about gender. It's the universal human quest for autonomy and growth.

3. **Fire Energy – The Longing for Connection:** Fire dances for warmth and togetherness. Its core soul question burns brightly: "Am I loved, valued, accepted?" Gender isn't even on the guest list. This is the shared human yearning for love and belonging.

4. **Earth Energy – The Search for Understanding:** Imagine earth, grounding and nurturing. It whispers its core soul question: "Do I understand? Am I understood?" This isn't about being a man or woman. It's about our shared need for comprehension and communication.

5. **Metal Energy – The Pursuit of Fulfilment:** Visualize metal, steadfast and resilient. Its core soul question lingers: "What is missing?" This isn't about gender. It's the universal human journey towards wholeness.

Isn't it fascinating how these quintessential human qualities couldn't care less about gender norms?

In chapter 18, I'll show you how you can use your results from The Vitality Test to see and understand people around you better by letting an AI platform like ChatGPT analyse and help you communicate with people from their windows to the world.

It's awe-inspiring to see the outcome of being able to communicate with another person in a way that they feel seen, safe, and understood.

Another "Feminine and Masculine" Construct Busted!

In *The Change Makers Podcast* episode #128, titled "Why Men Are NOT from Mars, and Women Are NOT from Venus," Nick and I dived deep into this persistent labelling, even regarding energies.

As we explored, we unveiled the nuances of the label "masculine and feminine energies," aligning perfectly with the essence of this chapter.

We uncovered how these constructs perpetuate stereotypes, breeding discord in relationships.

We looked deeply at books like *Men Are from Mars and Women Are from Venus* and how they fuel divisive gender labels.

Our dialogue transitioned into dissecting individual perceptions of these energies, illuminating the significance of valuing uniqueness over rigid gender-based labels.

Nick and I advocated adopting a more specific and non-gendered language, particularly when discussing desired be-haviours. These constructs were unveiled to have a profound impact not only on relationships but also on personal expression and professional diversity.

One open conversation opened the gender box at the BPW European Conference in Reykjavik.

I recall a memorable experience during my workshop at the European Conference for Business and Professional Women

BPW in Reykjavik, Iceland, in 2022. As I delved into the topic "What if you've been told a lie about your gender?" concerning societal constructs and their impact on our everyday lives, I invited attendees to question the assumptions that often box us in by our genders.

A lively conversation emerged, with one woman from Spain sharing her son's observation about his wife's seemingly natural aptitude for caring for their infant. In response, I acknowledged that while some women might possess innate caregiving skills, others, like me, had to learn the ropes of infant care.

To drive the point home, I asked the entire audience, comprised of women from various backgrounds: "How many of you are mothers?" Almost every hand shot up. And then I asked: "How many of you found that caring for your infants required learning and effort rather than being purely instinctual?" A significant majority of the hands remained raised.

The impact of this exercise was palpable. The woman who had posed the original question had a transformative moment as she looked around and recognised the shared experience of learning and adaptation among the women in the room. This interaction exemplifies how powerful it is to challenge gender norms and assumptions.

Can you spot how tightly our society clings to gender stereotypes?

But let's be honest. Does this stereotyping allow people to explore their passions and stand up as their authentic selves?

Is there room for them to grow into something better, bolder, and brighter in their unique way?

Honestly, I don't think so!

Here's where Nick's wisdom comes in. These points aren't about being men or women; they're about how we've learned to express ourselves in the intricate dance of life.

Our brains have nothing to do with our gender! Yes, you heard it! Every brain is unique!

In 2020, Nick and I interviewed Gina Rippon for *The Change Makers Podcast* (episode #116). She shared her research in her work as a British neurobiologist, feminist, and professor emeritus of cognitive neuroimaging at the Aston Brain Centre, Aston University, Birmingham. She talked about how her book *The Gendered Brain* reshapes our understanding of gender and the brain.

As a distinguished neurobiologist and unwavering feminist, Gina challenges the conventional notions that associate gender with distinct brain characteristics and binary views and sparks a nuanced understanding of human diversity. Her insights are a beacon, guiding us towards a future free from confining norms.

Her work has shown her that every brain is unique, defying the oversimplified binary perspective on gender by debunking the myth of rigid gender-based brain differences.

Gina emphasises that every brain is unique and different from every other brain. She rejects that men's and women's brains are identical or completely different. Gina believes that individuals should not be limited to identifying strictly as male or female, as there is a wide range of diversity in how brains develop and function.

She argues against gender stereotypes and assumptions, highlighting that not all women are authentically empathic and not all men are automatically skilled in math.

The Consequences of Black-and-White Thinking

Gina suggests that thinking in binary terms and accepting clear-cut differences is an outdated and limiting perspective.

Her insights remind us that societal norms and stereotypes have perpetuated a narrow view of gender, stifling the recognition of individual differences. Gina emphasises the need for a more nuanced approach to understanding human diversity.

In a world where gender expectations often constrain leadership, her work paves the way for a new era of inclusive leadership that transcends traditional boundaries and fosters a more equitable and diverse landscape.

Example of Things Shifting: Soft Skills Rebranded as Power Skills

In today's rapidly evolving society, a profound shift is occurring. What was once categorised as stereotypical women's traits, such as kindness, caring, collaboration, emotional intelligence, called "soft skills"—which back in the day was often dismissed as nonessential in business—is transforming remarkably.

Today, these skills are rebranded as "power skills," a rebranding initiative that transcends the confines of gender stereotypes. It's no longer about feminine or masculine; it's about nurturing skills that empower individuals to lead effectively.

This rebranding makes these skills more inclusive and sparks curiosity across all genders, encouraging everyone to harness their potential as leaders inspired by the limitless possibilities of "power skills."

We need to continue to clean up this mess!

The real trick is to embrace the swirling whirlwind of energy, dance to our own beat, and revel in the masterpiece of gender-blending beauty that defines us.

Ready to hit the dance floor?

CHAPTER 5

Liberating the Language: Speaking a New Dialogue

"Every conversation is a brushstroke on the canvas of change. We can transform perspectives, uplift hearts, and ignite possibilities with each word. Let's craft a dialogue that paints a world of equality, authenticity, and boundless growth, one conversation at a time." —Bev Hancock

Alright, brace yourself, because we're diving into a chapter like a linguistic treasure trove. It's all about how we wield words, the power of our language, and the art of fresh, empowering dialogue.

Language is a powerful tool that shapes our perception and interaction with the world. However, you might have experienced moments where our language fails to capture the diverse tapestry of human identity.

Consider my own story, one to which many women can relate. Back when I was the country manager for a menswear brand, in international meetings, I was constantly greeted with a resounding "gentlemen."

What's the problem, you might be asking yourself? I didn't feel included in that term. It was as if I didn't exist in those moments because I couldn't relate to being part of that group.

When our language plays favourites with one gender, it's like trying to dance to a one-sided beat. Half the team does the cha-cha while the other half does the tango!

It's a stark reminder of how language can inadvertently exclude individuals and their identities.

Shifting from "guys" to "people" or "teams" might seem minor, but its impact is immense. These old terms like "guys" or other gender-specific terms will unconsciously lead us back to a time when leadership tables were occupied solely by men.

Some people say, "Hey, 'guys' can mean talking to both men and women together."

Okay, if that's true, have you ever tried saying, "Look at the guys across the street. One is on their period, one is breastfeeding, and one is pregnant"?

Can you see how that paints a hilarious picture and shows the absurdity of using "guys" for everyone? Let's face it: our language needs a little makeover to catch up with reality, or we'll end up with seriously confused parties, and not the fun kind!

The Good News!

Leaders who transcend these gender boundaries will be at the forefront of change, mindfully choosing words and actions.

Not naturally a good communicator? Fear not!

Communication can encompass something other than your natural skill at dialogue or conversation. The critical point I want to make is the power you have within yourself to change that around for you.

A leader who leads beyond genders has to be able to communicate and influence people of all genders. It's a journey. All it requires is taking the first step.

During *The Change Makers Podcast* interviews while researching this book, I had one conversation around the power of communication, this time with the incredible Bev Hancock, which stuck with me.

You know her, right? She is the language maestro. Who can weave words like a wizard? Yep, that's the one.

So, I was chatting with Bev Hancock. We were diving into how she became the linguistic wizard she is today.

Her journey was not a stroll in the park. It's a tale of transformation that shines a light on the potency of words and how they can reshape our world.

Bev's story was not a linear path to greatness. It was about her striving to sculpt a future for her kids, stepping out of her comfort zone, and embracing new frontiers. As a single mom post-divorce, Bev was on a mission to forge her destiny beyond the defined roles and expectations society handed her.

And guess what weapon she brandished in this epic battle? The power of communication.

Tech prowess and the art of connection—those were her secret weapons. But beneath the surface, Bev had a profound love for relationships that ran deeper than the ocean. These connections formed her magic circle, where authenticity thrived like a wildflower in spring. She had to uncover who she was by shedding the skin of who she wasn't.

It's a journey that sounds like something from an adventure novel.

And that's not all. The communication journey wasn't just about climbing a mountain and reaching the summit. It was about setting foot on the path of uncharted territories, one conversation at a time.

I like to think of it as Bev's version of "figuring it out as you go." Conversations became her North Star, guiding her through the unknown, lighting up the dark alleys, and helping her make sense of a complex world.

In my enlightening conversation with Bev Hancock on the podcast, a story highlighted the paramount role of conversations in our lives.

Bev illuminated how nothing surpasses the importance of the exchanges we engage in. As we delved into this realisation, she painted a vivid picture of conversations guiding sailboats, steering us towards the shores of understanding and growth. Her insights illuminated how our words possess the potential to shape our future and that of others.

Using the Zulu word *sawubona,* which means "I see you," Bev offered a captivating metaphor. This single phrase embodies the power to create a transformative conversational space. By genuinely seeing and connecting with one another, we break free from the cycle of shallow discourse and instead unearth genuine value.

Bev's wisdom underscored that every word we choose, every moment of presence, weaves a collective tapestry of connection and unity.

Learning from Bev's narrative, we can integrate the essence of *sawubona* into our daily rituals as leaders who transcend gender boundaries. Embrace the concept of genuinely seeing others, not through labels or stereotypes, but as fellow humans on unique journeys.

Practice active listening and empathy, aiming to understand rather than assume. By incorporating this Zulu wisdom, we can reshape our interactions and foster a culture of genuine connection, compassion, and understanding. As leaders who lead beyond gender, this simple yet profound practice will enable us to transcend divisions, build bridges, and create a narrative of unity, significantly impacting our personal and professional lives.

Now, let's zoom out for a moment.

The language we use isn't just a string of words; it's like a magic wand we wield to reshape perceptions and mould realities. Every conversation and sentence becomes a brush-stroke on the canvas of change. It's about transforming the mundane into the extraordinary, turning stereotypes on their heads, and crafting a dialogue that champions equality and authenticity.

Imagine walking into a room, not just with a hello but with the power to reshape the atmosphere with your words. That's the magic we're discussing—turning everyday conversations into profound empowerment tools.

Imagine your spoken words as vibrant sailboats, steering others towards the welcoming shores of understanding and growth. Like a wizard of a lexicon, you infuse your words with energies that folks unconsciously soak up. People feel through your words who you are, how you operate, and if you are welcoming them into your world as a leader who leads beyond gender.

These words aren't just letters. They're the building blocks of your reputation and the cornerstone of your personal brand.

So, let's set sail on a linguistic adventure, where each word becomes a compass pointing towards a more mindful and resonant connection.

Now, let's distil the wisdom of this chapter into five takeaways that can be your guiding stars.

1. **Word Alchemy**: Choose your words like a master alchemist. Opt for phrases that uplift, inspire, and honour diverse perspectives. Your words set the tone for open conversations and inclusive dialogue.

2. **Elevate, Don't Diminish**: Words can elevate, and they can undermine. When you communicate, focus on celebrating strengths and qualities, building bridges instead of walls.

3. **Challenge Stereotypes**: Transform language into a weapon against stereotypes. Pay very close attention to your choice of words. Instead of echoing outdated norms, redefine roles, expectations, and possibilities with your comments.

4. **Inclusive Pronouns**: Embrace the power of inclusive language. Swapping "he" or "she" with "they" or "people" instead of "guys" creates space for all identities, contributing to a more inclusive world.

5. **Empower Others**: Your linguistic prowess isn't just about you; it's about empowering those around you. Build an environment of trust and active listening that encourages authentic expression.

Daily habits become part of who you authentically operate as!

Here's your action plan to infuse these takeaways into your everyday life:

- Start your day with a moment of intention, where you consciously engage with the people you interact with. Ask yourself: "Am I truly seeing and connecting with them?"

- Throughout the day, as conversations unfold, remind yourself of the power *sawubona* holds.

- Commit to intentionally using inclusive language in meetings, casual chats, or emails.

- Reflect on your word choices at day's end. Did you spark growth or unintentionally perpetuate stereotypes?

- Learn, adapt, and keep the conversation of change alive.

So, go on, unleash your linguistic superpowers.

Become a conductor of change through the spoken word.

And remember, every sentence you craft, every word you choose, is a brushstroke in the masterpiece of transformation. It's time to sculpt a new dialogue that breaks the chains of limiting language and empowers every voice to resonate.

Your words, my friend, are your wand. Let's cast the transformation spell together.

CHAPTER 6

Unleashing the Power of Humour: Infusing Lightness into Leadership

"Laughter isn't just a sound; it's a tool that leaders can wield to shape a brighter, more inclusive future. We open doors to camaraderie, creativity, and authentic connections by infusing humour into our leadership journey. Laughter transcends boundaries and welcomes diversity, allowing us to lead with a light-hearted spirit while creating spaces where everyone's unique strengths shine." —Wendy Watkins.

Hello, laughter architects!

We're about to embark on a journey through the corridors of leadership sprinkled with the magic of humour.

Humour and *Beyond Gender: The New Rules of Leadership* means allowing yourself to tickle your own funny bone regularly—at the same time, being aware your sense of humour might not be everybody's cup of tea, and that's fine.

Now, before we dive headfirst into the laughter pool, let's address a vital point.

What do I mean when I say "unleashing the power of humour"?

It's about allowing yourself and others around you to use humour positively while being aware and paying close attention to the reactions and nonreactions around you.

Humour isn't a one-size-fits-all cape that transforms every leader into a stand-up comedian.

Awareness of your type of humour is crucial.

Using humour as a shield to hide behind isn't what the new rules of leadership are all about.

It's much more about fostering genuine connections, boosting morale, and creating an inclusive atmosphere.

So, let's explore how humour can be the glue that binds teams together without losing sight of authenticity.

Example: I have an arid sense of humour and can easily fall into throwing a joke of sarcasm. At the same time, I've noticed times in a team meeting where sarcasm is flying like confetti, but there's a lingering discomfort in the air.

What is intended to be a moment of shared laughter can quickly become an unintentional jab at someone's expense.

This is where the rubber meets the road. Leaders who transcend gender roles must understand the importance of humour that uplifts instead of undermines.

Let's break down three scenarios where gender sarcasm often comes into play and what leaders beyond genders do instead.

Scenario 1:

The Gender-Based Jibe: Picture the scene. A colleague walks into the room wearing a colourful tie that doesn't fit standard office attire. Instead of playful camaraderie, someone quips, "Nice tie. Is it the latest in the 'men's fashion disaster' collection?"

Laughter erupts, but beneath the surface, the targeted colleague might feel more self-conscious than amused.

A "New Rules of Leadership" Approach: Our leader acknowledges the tie with genuine interest: *"Hey, nice tie! I like how it adds colour to our sea of neutrals."*

The atmosphere remains light, and the colleague's unique style is celebrated rather than ridiculed. This way, humour becomes a bridge, connecting people through positive appreciation.

Scenario 2:

The Snide Gender Comparison: During a brainstorming session, someone playfully suggests that women are inherently better at multitasking than men. Laughter fills the room, but beneath the chuckles, the reinforcement of gender stereotypes seeps in.

A "New Rules of Leadership" Approach: Our leader seizes the moment, "Ah, the age-old debate of multitasking! But you know what? Regardless of our chromosomes, we're all rock stars at juggling tasks here."

The conversation shifts from a gender-based comparison to celebrating everyone's abilities, reminding everyone that their skills are what matter, not their gender.

Scenario 3:

The Undermining Gender Gag: In a casual conversation, a lighthearted remark is made about how "real men" don't understand complex emotions. Laughs follow, but the perpetuation of the emotionally distant male stereotype might linger.

A Leader Beyond Genders Approach: Our leader chimes in, "I've met plenty of 'real men' who are fantastic at understanding emotions and expressing themselves. It's all about being human, right?"

The conversation reframes the narrative, reminding everyone that emotional intelligence knows no gender boundaries.

Incorporating humour into leadership isn't about tiptoeing around sensitive topics. It's about using humour to bridge gaps, build rapport, and create a comfortable space for authentic connections. It's essential to be attuned to the impact of our words and the underlying messages they convey.

A leader who follows the "new rule of leadership" harnesses humour to build unity, foster inclusivity, and encourage open dialogue.

So, let's make a pact: Practice leading with humour that uplifts, enlightens, and unites. Strive to refrain from using humour as a smokescreen for perpetuating outdated stereotypes.

Instead, let's infuse our leadership with humour as diverse as our team members, celebrating their uniqueness and encouraging a shared sense of joy.

Have humour for yourself!

The first step in this critical process is to have humour for yourself!

Being able to laugh at your own flaws and mistakes is a skill set that can help you create a culture around you that enables people to:

- Openly admit to their mistakes on their way

- Create a culture that's light and open

In the vibrant tapestry of transformative leadership, the ability to laugh at ourselves is pivotal. It's not just about sharing a hearty chuckle; it's about humbling ourselves, especially when we inadvertently stumble into the pit of labelling people by our unconscious biases.

Picture this scenario: You assume that the guy in his twenties knows all about the latest software, or you reach out to your female colleague and ask if you can borrow some hand lotion. These are some preferences or capabilities based on preconceived notions of gender. When you discover that the guy knows less about software than you do, or the girl has never used hand lotion, you see your assumptions are not true.

Instead of letting embarrassment take over, "Leaders Beyond Genders" embrace a lighthearted perspective.

- You can laugh at your unconscious biases and excuse yourself by saying, "Sorry, I think I just put you into a box."

- You recognise that even the most well-intentioned minds can slip into the biased territory.

- By doing so, you start to foster an atmosphere of openness and growth by sharing a laugh at your own expense and acknowledging the slipup.

It's like a reset button that allows you to reframe your thinking and forge ahead with a renewed commitment to unbiased leadership.

As we journey through the terrain of leadership, let's remember that humour is a multifaceted gem—it has the power to entertain, connect, and inspire.

Can CFOs be funny and professional at the same time?

Allow me to share a remarkable story that exemplifies the transformative power of infusing humour into one's leadership journey.

One of my clients, a seasoned CFO in a prominent insurance company, embarked on a 360-degree personal brand assessment with me. As we delved into the perceptions of those around him, a fascinating dichotomy emerged. While his family and friends cherished his playful and humorous side, his colleagues and subordinates at work primarily saw him as a serious and hardworking professional.

This revelation triggered a profound reflection for him. He began questioning why he had been compartmentalising his authentic self, suppressing the humour that came naturally to him in his professional life. With newfound awareness, he intended to bridge this gap and bring his genuine self to work.

We witnessed a remarkable shift during our follow-up assessment six months later. The feedback from colleagues and subordinates indicated a notable change. They now recognised his humour and approachability.

What was most striking, however, was his own testimonial. He expressed how much more he was relishing his work, no longer constrained by the belief that a CFO in the insurance sector must maintain an unyielding seriousness. This transformation illustrated the profound impact of embracing authenticity and humour.

His self-discovery journey allowed him to break free from societal conditioning and develop a leadership style aligned with his true essence. His story underlines the importance of self-awareness and the transformative potential of infusing lightness and humour into one's professional life, ultimately enhancing joy, connection, and fulfilment in leadership.

Practical Exercises to Infuse Humour into Your Leadership Journey

As we conclude this chapter, I invite you to roll up your sleeves and dive into practical exercises that will empower you to infuse humour into your leadership journey.

Let's start with a classic: the **"Humour Challenge."**

Identify three upcoming situations in your professional life where tension might be high, or creativity might need a boost. Then, brainstorm three humorous icebreakers, anecdotes, or playful comments that could serve as conversation starters or mood lighteners in those moments.

Shifting gears to your personal life, try the **"Laughter Mirror."** For a week, make a conscious effort to find humour in everyday situations, be it a minor mishap or a playful observation.

Jot down your funny encounters in a journal each evening and reflect on how they made you feel.

Lastly, embrace the **"Comedy Remix."** Choose a familiar, perhaps mundane, process in your team or family and reimagine it with a humorous twist. Brainstorm how to incorporate wordplay, funny props, or amusing visuals to liven up the experience. These exercises will foster creativity and empower you to lead with a light touch, cultivating an environment where authenticity and joy thrive.

So, dear leaders of tomorrow, let your laughter echo through the hallways of your leadership journey, creating an environment where authenticity and humour dance harmoniously.

After all, authentic leadership isn't just about steering the ship; it's about setting a course filled with moments of laughter and genuine connections.

CHAPTER 7

Navigating the Gender Obstacle Course: Overcoming Challenges with Grace

"Embrace the Power of Small Shifts: With every choice, every step, you're moulding your mind. Like a sculptor each small change shapes new pathways, leading you toward the boundless realm of self-discovery and transformation."
—Dr. David Paul

Welcome to the obstacle part of implementing the new rules of leadership! As we embark on this exhilarating journey, gear up to navigate the twists, turns, and hurdles that come our way.

This chapter is about tackling the challenges head-on, equipped with resilience and grace. From biases lurking in the shadows to societal norms we've outgrown, we're about to provide ourselves with strategies that will make us champions of inclusive leadership. So, are you ready to take the lead in demolishing these barriers? Let's lace up our mindfulness shoes and embark on this transformative adventure.

In our quest, let's pause to explore the incredible story shared by Dr. David Paul, or Dr. David as I call him, who I interviewed in my research for *The Change Makers Podcast—Leadership Beyond Gender* series, episode #149.

Dr. David recounted a tale of triumph over adversity, revealing how he harnessed the power of mindfulness to rise above pain and loss.

Through mindfulness, he overcame the heart-wrenching aftermath of a car accident that tragically claimed his brother's life. His journey is a testament to the resilience that mindfulness can instil within us, allowing us to navigate the most challenging terrains with grace and composure.

Armed with his neuroscience wisdom, Dr. David brings a groundbreaking revelation to our journey. He explains how making small, conscious changes in our daily lives can rewire our brain's neural pathways. It could be as little as taking a left turn in an intersection where you usually take a right turn. Even a small change like that will light up your brain, creating new pathways.

Much like training a new muscle, practising mindfulness and meditation cultivates self-awareness. Imagine this as a mental gym where you're building the muscles needed to lead beyond gender.

Change challenge to opportunities!

Dr. David's perspective is a revelation that reframes how we perceive the hurdles we encounter on our journey to seeing people for who they authentically are, not by the box we've placed them into.

His call to stop labelling these obstacles as mere **"challenges"** and instead view them as **"opportunities"** for transformation reshapes the landscape of our mindset.

Imagine the seismic shift this language change could bring about in our minds—a transformation from perceiving difficulties as roadblocks to embracing them as catalysts for growth.

When we internalise this shift, our minds undergo a metamorphosis. Instead of feeling weighed down by challenges, we find ourselves energised by the prospect of change, guided by optimism and a sense of purpose.

This cognitive shift ushers in a cascade of positive effects in our day-to-day lives.

Firstly, our resilience and adaptability soar. No longer daunted by challenges, we approach them with a renewed spirit, ready to innovate and overcome.

Secondly, our interactions with others become more collaborative and constructive. This new perspective fosters empathy, encouraging us to see problems from diverse angles and seek collective solutions.

Finally, this change in mindset infuses our actions with intentionality. We become architects of change, proactively seeking opportunities to reshape the world.

Embracing his insight, we redefine our relationship with challenges and set off a ripple effect that touches every aspect of our lives.

Become adept at recognising your unconscious biases!

By doing things differently and mindfully, we become adept at recognising our unconscious biases—all 188 of them! These insights empower us to choose our responses, ensuring they align with our true selves and our mission as leaders.

As you embark on this transformative journey, remember that each step taken mindfully is a stride towards the leader you're destined to be. Much like training a new muscle, you're building a mental strength that will set you apart.

With mindfulness as your secret weapon, you're not just breaking gender moulds. You're crafting a new narrative. Your voice, actions, and intentions become beacons of authentic leadership that guide others beyond the confining walls of gender norms.

Dr. David's insights hold significant value for leaders propelling themselves and others beyond gender confines. Much like being guided through uncharted terrain, his revelation that the brain thrives on change suggests a potent strategy.

Leaders keen on transcending gender norms must employ this wisdom as a tool. Deliberately breaking routine patterns enables their minds to forge fresh neural pathways, enhancing neuroplasticity.

This practice fuels cognitive expansion, allowing leaders to approach challenges from novel angles. Dr. David's emphasis on escaping stagnant routines illuminates the path to unlocking the brain's full potential.

For leaders orchestrating change beyond gender, this neurological principle becomes a beacon.

As they navigate the obstacle course of gender bias, societal norms, and resilience, this approach becomes instrumental.

Just as a seasoned runner adjusts their stride for different obstacles, leaders recalibrate their neural responses for diverse situations. They turn "challenges" into opportunities. The process of forging new mental connections mirrors the journey they're pioneering—one that transcends conventional gender boundaries.

Through mindful adaptation and conscious choices, leaders embody the transformative power of Dr. David's revelation, propelling themselves and their teams towards an inclusive, boundary-defying future.

Now, let's decode the takeaways that will become your compass on this journey.

1. **Embrace the Mindful Mindset:** Treat each morning as a fresh start by setting aside a few minutes for mindfulness meditation. Close your eyes, focus on

your breath, and let your thoughts flow without judgement. This practice will become the compass guiding you through the gender obstacle course of the day, helping you approach challenges with a clear and centred mind.

2. **Recognise and Redirect Biases:** Practice "bias checkpoints." Whenever you notice a judgement or assumption about someone based on gender, pause, and ask yourself, "Is this bias accurate, or can I choose a more open-minded perspective?" Challenge yourself to replace biased thoughts with inclusive ones, gradually training your mind to respond with empathy.

3. **Challenge Societal Norms:** I've said this before and will repeat it. Select a societal norm you feel particularly passionate about challenging. It could be in the workplace, home, or social settings. Commit to speaking up whenever you see this norm being reinforced. Your willingness to stand tall and advocate for inclusive leadership will inspire others to question the status quo.

4. **Harness the Power of Resilience:** Introduce a "resilience checkpoint" during challenging moments. When faced with adversity, take a deep breath, and remind yourself that challenges are growth opportunities. Practice shifting your perspective by asking, "Where is the opportunity within this situation?"

5. **Daily Mindfulness Routine:** Begin each day with a mindful ritual. Find a quiet space, light a candle, and sit comfortably. Engage in deep breathing, letting go of any tension or stress. Then, reflect on your intentions for the day, focusing on your authentic

leadership journey beyond gender. Set positive affirmations that align with your purpose and visualise yourself confidently navigating the gender obstacle course.

By incorporating these daily habits into your routine, you're training your mental muscles and reinforcing the foundations of the new leadership rules—leading beyond gender. Each practice contributes to your growth as a trailblazer who leads authentically, challenges biases, and paves the way for a more inclusive and empowered world.

Breaking Down Barriers: Navigating Gender Obstacles with Self-Awareness, Self-Leadership, and Humour

In this uncharted territory of leadership beyond gender, we must acknowledge that there will be obstacles, strong currents pulling us back into the safety of old paradigms. Forces determined to uphold stereotypical gender roles may attempt to shroud our journey with doubt, scepticism, or resistance.

These elements can come in various forms, from subtle societal norms to overt pushback from those uncomfortable with change.

Example: the well-meaning colleague who dismisses your ideas due to ingrained gender biases, the boardroom dynamics that inadvertently silence diverse voices, the persistent societal expectations that nudge you back into conventional roles, the media narratives that continue to perpetuate outdated stereotypes, and even the self-doubt that occasionally creeps in as you challenge the status quo.

Overcoming Your Fear on this Journey

Doing things differently than what might be seen as the norm will bring up fear. The trick is not to believe in fear!

When I asked Dr. David about the concept of fear that will arise for many, he delved into the realm of fear and its impact on change, offering invaluable insights on how to conquer it and embrace transformation.

Our fear comes from our perceptions rather than actualities.

He underscores fear's tendency to stem from perceptions rather than actualities, advocating for re-valuating and reshaping these perceptions.

Dr. David illuminates how fear often thrives in the face of the unknown, yet he suggests a paradigm shift that frames uncertainty as an exciting avenue for growth. He underscores the pivotal role of action in overcoming fear, as taking deliberate steps weakens fear's grip and bolsters our inner fortitude.

Based on his wisdom gleaned from years of research and work in the field of complex large-scale change, Dr David points out that by dismantling limiting beliefs, welcoming the uncharted course, and embarking on purposeful, incremental steps, we equip ourselves to embrace change despite fear's presence.

Therefore, I say: Fear not, my friend! For you possess a formidable arsenal to dismantle these hurdles. Self-awareness becomes your compass, guiding you through biases and resistance. Armed with a strong self-leadership, you remain grounded even when faced with opposition.

And let's not forget the power of humour, as I talked about in chapter 6. Humour can be your secret weapon to disarm the gravity of these situations.

Just as a sprinter leap over hurdles with grace and agility, you, as a leader beyond gender, can gracefully navigate these challenges.

Remember, every chuckle at an absurd gender stereotype is a step forward; every witty retort to an outdated comment is a stride towards progress.

Your journey to defy these obstacles becomes a testament to your commitment, resilience, and authenticity.

Embrace the power of your uniqueness, and with self-awareness, self-leadership, and humour as your allies, you'll vault over these hurdles with a confidence and clarity that shines brighter than any gender-based limitation.

As we navigate the intricate labyrinth of challenges on the path to implementing the new leadership rules, let us remember that the obstacles we overcome today are the stepping-stones to a future free from the constraints of gender stereotypes.

As we dismantle one barrier at a time, we chip away at the walls that confine us to prescribed roles and limitations. With each triumph over adversity, we pave the way for a world where every individual can rise, unburdened by the weight of societal norms.

Let these triumphs become the symbols of our determination to shatter the gender obstacles that have persisted for far too long. For in our tenacity lies the promise of a future where leadership knows no bounds, and gender is but a footnote in the grand tapestry of our collective potential.

CHAPTER 8

The Power of Allies: Uniting for Change

"Gender equality starts at the kitchen table, where open conversations brew ideas, simmer beliefs, and cook up a world where every voice matters, and every heart is nourished." —Thordís Lóa Thorhallsdóttir

The truth becomes strikingly evident in change-making; actual change happens when we stand united.

In this chapter, we're about to explore the exhilarating journey of finding new alleys in pursuing the new rules of leadership in a messed-up world.

This chapter is not just an exploration—it's a call to action. It's a rallying cry for individuals of all genders to unite, support each other, and amplify our diverse voices for a future without gender boundaries.

If Iceland can bring gender equality, why not in your home, business, organisation, community, or country?

Picture this: a small island nation with a little less than 400,000 inhabitants, surrounded by the vast expanse of the North Atlantic Ocean, where the forces of nature converge with the tenacity of its people to shape a society that champions equality.

Welcome to Iceland—my home country, a country that is often seen as the extraordinary crucible where the temperature is not the only hot thing. Iceland's historic triumph for gender equality throughout the last century has been nothing short of a blazing trail that has ignited minds and hearts across the globe.

Let's dive into the heart of the Icelandic Gender Equality Model, the cousin of the Nordic Gender Equality Model. This innovative approach is a true testament to what can be achieved when a society unites with purpose.

It's a dynamic blend of policies, regulations, and cultural shifts aimed at dismantling gender barriers and fostering an environment where every individual has the freedom to flourish. This model has unleashed a tidal wave of change, impacting women and men as they embrace roles and responsibilities beyond traditional norms.

Here's a glimpse of what has been achieved in Iceland so far.

- Paid parental leaves for both parents; twelve months in total. If fathers don't take their part of the leave, it does not move over to the mothers.

- Businesses and organisations need certification to show equal pay is executed.

- Over 85 percent of women work outside their homes.

- More women than men graduate from universities.

- The public media RUV holds a gender bookkeeping sheet. They consciously ensure that all genders get equal exposure in their TV programs.

- Every year, a privately owned company displays the balance between genders in the media. This has become a great PR opportunity for the media, which consciously ensures people of all genders are given space to share their thoughts and knowledge.

The list above is only a fraction of what Icelanders see as "normal" today.

In addition to the above-mentioned list, the Icelandic naming system based upon Viking traditions gives space for individuality.

Let's delve into a unique facet of Icelandic culture—our naming system. In Iceland, we don't carry traditional family names. Instead, our surnames are derived from our parents' first names, suffixed with "dottir" (daughter) or "son."

For instance, my name, Runa Magnusdottir, reveals that my father's first name is Magnus, making me Magnus's daughter. I could use my mother's first name, Ingibjorg, adding "dottir" behind her first name. Using your father's first name is more common. This naming tradition underscores our emphasis on individuality, setting us apart from the conventional Mr. and Mrs. titles.

Let's say I was married to a man named Jonsson, son of Jon. I would still be Magnusdottir because I'm not the son of Jon.

Try it for yourself.

Take your parent's first name (it doesn't matter if you take your mother's first name or father's first name).

Write down your first name, then your parent's first name, and end with either 'dottir' or 'son' depending on your gender.

Do that for all members of your family. If you have children, look at how their names will also change.

List all the "new" names and notice how their identity and individuality change.

Do you see now how one naming system can change your identity?

The Challenges We Face in Iceland

The effect of the Gender Equality Model reverberates through-out every corner of Icelandic society. It's not just about legislative checkboxes or political correctness; it's about offering a lifestyle where men and women share the stage, collaborate as equals, and create a symphony of progress. This model's profound impact lies in its unwavering commitment to bridging the gender gap and rewriting the leadership narrative.

But let's get real. Change doesn't happen overnight. The Gender Equality Model is not without its challenges.

Even in a country known for gender equality, deeply ingrained biases persist. Thordis Loa Thorhallsdottir, or Loa as I call her, a dear friend, and a trailblazing leader both in the political world and in gender equality and inclusive practices, sheds light on this in a powerful episode of *The Change Makers Podcast*, episode #148.

She underscores how biases can seep into language, body language, and societal structures. The issue of men controlling money and networks behind the scenes serves as a hidden problem, demanding recognition, and resolution.

Loa also raises the curtain on the necessity of changing power dynamics. She emphasises that true gender equality requires a shift in the web of connections and power. Laws may need fine-tuning, and quotas may need to be introduced to rectify the gender imbalance. The key is recognising our biases and not letting them define the truth. Social conditioning clouds our perception, inhibiting the world from reaching its fullest potential.

The change starts at the kitchen table!

Beyond politics and public discourse, Loa directs our attention to a unique battleground for change—the kitchen table.

Conversations and decisions about life, family, and society should commence here.

Just think about how it can affect the conversations at your dinner table when you discover what matters to you and your family members and can talk about what matters to each family member.

That's inclusive conversations and inclusive decision-making.

What could the topics be about? Here are five ideas.

Five Different Kinds of Kitchen Table Conversations

1. **Shared Responsibilities:** Discuss how household chores and caregiving tasks are divided within the family. Explore ways to ensure everyone participates equally in maintaining the home and caring for one another, regardless of traditional gender roles.

   The questions to discuss: "What do you want our home to look and feel like? What matters most to you?" It could also bring in more creativity and fun whilst doing the laundry, clearing the house, etc. Allow every family member to come up with their own ideas.

2. **Career Aspirations:** Encourage open conversations about career goals and aspirations for all family members. Address any stereotypes or biases influencing these aspirations and brainstorm ways to support each individual's dreams.

   The question you could bring to the kitchen table could be: "Imagine if we could have any job in the world— real or fantasy! What would it be and why?" Add a touch of whimsy: encourage family members to dream big and explore unconventional career ideas. Exchange funny anecdotes about the wildest job ambitions. Then, dive into discussions about how to support each other's dreams. Notice when old stereotypes of gender roles kick in and point them out.

3. **Media and Gender:** Explore how media influences perceptions of gender roles and bodies. Discuss the portrayals of men and women in movies, TV shows, and advertisements. Analyse these depictions and reflect on how they may affect perceptions within the family and society.

    The discussion point could be: "What's the funniest or most ridiculous gender stereotype you've seen in a movie or TV show?" Discuss how such images are unrealistic and what positive representations could look like. Remember, real life isn't a sitcom!

4. **Financial Literacy:** Imagine if you spent some time talking about finances at the dinner table, not from a place of lack but with a conversation that sparks interest. Teach financial literacy and decision-making skills by involving all family members in budget discussions and financial planning. Emphasise the importance of financial independence and understanding for everyone, regardless of gender.

    A topic you could initiate for a conversation could be: "If you could invent a new currency that's not money, what would it be? And how would you earn it?" Inject some playfulness: explore creative ideas for alternative currencies (like kindness coins or adventure points). Transition to a chat about money management, savings, and why financial independence is as exciting as discovering hidden treasures.

5. **Inclusive Decision-Making:** Practice making family decisions together, involving each member regardless of age or gender. Teach the value of listening to different perspectives, fostering empathy, and respecting each other's choices.

   A conversation could be around the question: *"If our family were to invent a brand-new holiday tradition, what would it be?"* Spark imagination: discuss imaginative and fun traditions that every family member would enjoy. Transition to discussing the importance of including everyone's ideas in family decisions, just like creating new holiday traditions together.

By blending humour, creativity, and lightheartedness into these kitchen table conversations, families can not only promote gender equality but also create cherished memories filled with laughter and connection.

The impact of Iceland's model transcends personal lives is an investment in society itself.

In this *Change Makers Podcast* episode with Loa, she asserts that gender equality should be a win-win scenario, benefiting all. Its investment should be supported through taxation, leading to improved macroeconomic performance, better lives, and enhanced opportunities for everyone. The challenge lies in catalysing action and structurally implementing tools and laws.

Media and societal attitudes also come under scrutiny. The media plays a role in shaping societal perceptions of gender. Adaptation to a new era, where gender is less rigidly defined, is essential.

Equality should be a thread woven into the fabric of society, government, and municipalities. To lead beyond gender, you must advocate for an organisation offering welfare and childcare for all, transcending specific groups.

The message is clear: investing in equality is as vital as investing in areas like welfare and infrastructure—the **Icelandic Gender Equality Model.**

The Icelandic Gender Equality Model is a beacon of progress, weaving legislative innovation, cultural transformation, and individual commitment into a tapestry of true equality. This dynamic framework dismantles gender barriers, nurturing an environment where every person, regardless of gender, can thrive and contribute without constraints. Rooted in inclusive policies, diverse representation, and shared responsibilities, the model challenges many traditional norms and paves the way for a society where leadership is defined by capability, not gender.

The Icelandic Gender Equality Model can set an example for the world and testify to the power of collective action in shaping a more inclusive and equitable future.

Facing the Facts

When it comes to legislation, gender equality is here in Iceland.

However, this is a big issue: for the bill to work as intended, we must look closely at our unconscious biases, habits, and rituals to enable strong leadership that can lead beyond genders.

So, how does Iceland's experience influence our perception of gender equality today?

Here are six things considered normal in Iceland but which stretch the boundaries of convention in many other countries:

1. **Shared Parental Leave:** In Iceland, paid parental leave is not just for mothers. Fathers actively

participate in parenting by taking shared parental leave, setting a new standard for family dynamics. This legislation moved the needle forward. With paid parental leave for both parents, it doesn't matter today if you are a man or a woman seeking high workplace positions at the age you might want to start a family. The employer knows both partners will take a leave of absence—not just the mother—therefore women aren't passed over for promotions or given less responsibility because they may have children and take parental leave.

2. **Gender-Neutral Language:** The Icelandic language is working hard to become more gender-neutral, embracing inclusivity rather than reinforcing binary norms. We are not there yet and are making many mistakes, but changes are happening.

3. **Diverse Representation:** Iceland boasts one of the highest percentages of women in the workforce and leadership roles in the public sector. The private sector for CEO roles is getting there, just slower.

4. **Inclusive Corporate Culture:** Icelandic companies increasingly prioritise gender equality in leadership positions, creating a culture where women have equal opportunities to ascend the corporate ladder.

5. **All Genders Are Invited to the Conversation:** More men are opening up and seeing the benefits for themselves valuing their nurturing part of themselves and thoroughly enjoying fatherhood, not just as the provider but as a caring, fostering father who does just about everything except giving birth to the child or breastfeeding (obviously).

6. **Championing Women's Rights Globally:** Iceland consistently ranks at the forefront in global gender equality indices, setting an example for nations worldwide.

I often hear people outside Iceland say, "Iceland is heaven for women!" I see it differently. The Icelandic Gender Equality model isn't just helping women; it's serving the nation.

In my ideal world, I would love to see these shifts, seemingly ordinary in Iceland today, send ripples across the globe.

Leaders who apply the new leadership rules will think about what can be achieved and use that to inspire what they want to see change within their families, communities, businesses, or organisations.

Let this proof that it can be done show us what can be achieved when individuals unite to pursue equality and leadership beyond gender. Iceland's journey teaches us that change happens not just through top-down policies but also through inclusive conversations, individual commitments, and a collective drive for progress.

The Icelandic Gender Equality Model should spark the fire of transformation, demonstrating that actual change is not just possible—it's inevitable when we stand united.

Let's be clear about one vitally important thing. Iceland wasn't always this way! Oh no. Iceland was once a replica of the general patriarchal system, and we are still slaves to that old system. We are still talking about women's roles, jobs. We are still referring to women as a minority group.

However, we have moved the needle forward more perhaps than other countries.

Applying the New Rules of Leadership Beyond Gender

How about we ditch the monochrome lens and adopt a full-spectrum view? Let's pop the gender box wide open and invite anyone who's fed up with the status quo to join the revolution. Instead of segregating the dialogue, let's make it a melting pot of perspectives and possibly, just maybe, inch closer to closing that stubborn gender gap for good.

Let's add a twist to the narrative. What if Iceland became the catalyst for a global revolution that breaks free from the archaic boxes we've been stuck in? Imagine the seismic shift if we brought everyone to the table—men, women, and non-binary folks—each with unique gifts to confront issues like sexual violence and the gender pay gap.

Instead of a singular rallying cry from one side of the fence, we'd have a harmonised chorus that can't be ignored. No more throwing stones; we're all in the same glass house.

This united front would not only supercharge Iceland's progress but also set a new global standard. A standard that says, "Hey, we're better together. Let's fix this." It's not just a women's or men's issue; it's our society's issue, a human issue. And solving human issues requires the full spectrum of humanity.

Such a move could ripple through the world, challenging the status quo and making folks question why they're still upholding divisions that only keep us stagnant. You bet it'd make heads spin, but more importantly, it would open minds.

That's where the new leadership rules, beyond gender, apply.

Keep that in mind, and I encourage you to ask yourself: "If the people in Iceland could make things happen, how can I make it my inspiration to strive for a future in my world where people around me can thrive unapologetically?"

The Challenges You Will Face as a Leader Advocating for a Better World for All Genders

In chapter 4, I told you about the interview I and Nick Haines had with Gina Rippon, the author of *The Gendered Mind*, exploring how new neuroscience explodes the myths of the male and female minds in 2020.

Gina's research insights play a significant role in the ever-evolving leadership landscape beyond genders. Her profound insights on the ongoing debate surrounding gender identity and self-identification serve as a beacon of wisdom and empowerment.

Despite the latest neuroscience and epigenetic research showing that the difference between men and women isn't about their brains but their internal programs created by their upbringing, environment, habits, and rituals, humanity is stuck in socially constructed boxes.

As leaders poised to break free from the confines of traditional gender norms and unleash people's superpowers regardless of their genders, we face various challenges that demand innovative solutions and collaborative efforts.

Looking at Gina's perspectives sheds light on three significant challenges that leaders navigating this path might encounter, offering guidance on overcoming them through her nuanced understanding.

We Are Confronting Societal Norms and Expectations

Firstly, the challenge of confronting societal norms and expectations looms large. Gina's assertion that who we are is not solely tethered to our biological components challenges the foundation of traditional gender constructs.

To overcome this challenge, leaders can embrace Gina's wisdom by actively advocating for an inclusive environment that encourages individuals to explore their authentic selves.

By fostering an atmosphere of acceptance, leaders can inspire their teams to question norms and embrace diversity.

Perpetuation of Harmful Gender Stereotypes

Secondly, the perpetuation of harmful gender stereotypes poses a significant hurdle.

In Gina's podcast interview, she emphasised that the negative consequences of these stereotypes—whether on professions, disciplines, or mental health—underscores the urgency of addressing this issue.

As leaders beyond genders, we can utilise her insights by initiating conversations that challenge such stereotypes and actively promoting diverse representation across all levels of leadership.

We must be aware of our unconscious biases and question our reactions and judgements. We can always make it our intention to set a powerful example for others by championing a culture that values individuality over conformity.

Resistance from Those Invested in Maintaining the Status Quo

Lastly, leaders striving for change beyond genders might encounter resistance from those invested in maintaining the status quo. Sometimes, research findings don't rise to the surface as clearly as others.

Despite inconclusive research findings, Rippon's recognition of the strong desire to uphold clear-cut differences between genders resonates deeply.

To navigate this challenge, leaders can draw on Rippon's advocacy for shifting societal attitudes. By creating safe spaces for open dialogue and education, leaders can gradually shift perspectives and encourage a collective effort to dismantle rigid gender norms.

By confronting societal norms, challenging stereotypes, and rallying allies, leaders can foster an environment where authenticity thrives, diversity is celebrated, and individuals are valued for who they are. Gina Rippon's wisdom and research results testify to the transformative power of collaboration in pursuing leadership that transcends the limitations of gender.

You and I can create a ripple effect within our world, starting with our families. Let's build a future where gender equality is not an exception but the norm—a norm that transcends borders, shatters boundaries, and ushers in a new era of leadership that knows no gender limits.

In conclusion, "Chapter 8, The Power of Allies: Uniting for Change," beckons us to recognise that the strength of change lies in unity. This chapter has taken us on a journey exploring the invaluable role of allies in pursuing the new leadership rules.

We've drawn inspiration from Iceland's remarkable journey towards gender equality—grounded in fostering alliances, championing diverse voices, and collectively rewriting the norms that shape our lives.

We've delved into the heart of transformation, discovering that change starts right at the kitchen table, where open conversations ignite ideas, reshape beliefs, and pave the path to a world where every voice finds its place and every heart is nourished.

Thordís Lóa Thorhallsdóttir's poignant words resonate deeply: "Gender equality starts at the kitchen table, where open conversations brew ideas, simmer beliefs, and cook up a world where every voice matters, and every heart is nourished."

The actual change isn't confined to policymaking chambers or public debates. It starts where personal lives intersect in homes, families, and intimate conversations. It's in these spaces that stereotypes and biases are dismantled and a foundation of equality is built.

The story of the woman from Spain, her poignant question about her son's observation, and the subsequent revelation that infant care doesn't come naturally to everyone illustrates the potential of these conversations to evoke transformation.

By challenging societal norms and delving into these discussions, we spark a shift in perspective that recognises shared experiences, questions deeply ingrained beliefs, and paves the way for a more inclusive future.

The power of these kitchen table conversations transcends personal lives—a ripple that spreads outward, influencing communities, workplaces, and society.

The Icelandic Gender Equality Model underscores that equality isn't an isolated achievement but an investment in societal well-being. It reminds us that change isn't a solitary endeavour; it's a collective commitment to challenge biases, question norms, and create a world where every individual thrives.

The journey of change isn't without its challenges, and Thordís Loa Thorhallsdóttir's interview highlights some of these hurdles. Biases that seep into language and societal structures and the need to change power dynamics serve as reminders that the journey towards gender equality requires sustained effort. Yet, as we navigate these challenges, we're guided by the understanding that equality begins in conversations that empower individuals to see beyond traditional roles and definitions.

The kitchen table conversations bring change home, quite literally. They challenge the status quo, rewrite family dynamics, and foster a culture where diversity is celebrated and individuality flourishes. Through the lens of Iceland's journey and the transformative potential of these conversations, we glimpse the future. In this world, leadership knows no gender limits, where authenticity and equality are cherished, and where unity propels us towards lasting change.

The time to unite for change is now, and as we embark on this journey, let us remember that change happens not just in grand gestures but in the everyday conversations we have with our loved ones.

Let's keep the flame of inspiration alive, igniting it within our own spheres of influence and sparking a movement that reshapes the narrative of leadership beyond gender.

With every dialogue, every perspective shared, and every heart opened, we inch closer to a world where unity, equality, and transformation reign supreme.

The time to unite for change is now.

Chapter 9

Embracing Vulnerability:
The Key to Authentic Connection

*"Vulnerability isn't a weakness to hide;
it's a doorway to our greatest strengths.
When we embrace our vulnerabilities,
we cultivate the courage to stand authentically
resiliently, and passionately.
Our journey from struggle to strength
becomes a beacon of inspiration,
lighting the path for others to follow."*
—Bev Hancock

In vulnerability, the strength of a true leader emerges. Welcome to a chapter about shedding pretence and uncovering the gold beneath—our authenticity.

It's time to dive into the often-overlooked wellspring of leadership: vulnerability.

Let's start with a powerhouse author, researcher, and lecturer named Brené Brown. She's like the vulnerability guru, the high priestess of authenticity.

Bréne Brown's research unearthed the remarkable truth: vulnerability isn't a sign of weakness but a display of courage. It's a cornerstone of authentic leadership, allowing us to connect profoundly. Imagine that; instead of pretending to be the all-knowing fortress, we open up about our uncertainties and fears. It's like discovering a hidden superpower, and it's the stuff that legendary leaders are made of.

Or look at Oprah Winfrey—the ultimate queen of conversation. In her heart-to-heart interviews with Michelle Obama, a powerful revelation shines through. Michelle and Oprah radiate leadership and agree that vulnerability is the bridge to genuine connection. They're talking about breaking the mask and speaking from the heart, even when it's uncomfortable. It's in these moments that authentic leadership ignites.

Men don't show emotions, ergo, they are emotionless.

Speaking of masks, let's chat about the gender box society has crafted around vulnerability—the box that allows women to express vulnerability more freely than men.

I recall being acutely aware of my biases and behaviours towards men. I had unknowingly bought into the stereotype that men were emotionless, and I, in turn, treated them as such. I cracked jokes, poked fun, and laughed at them rather than with them. It was a profound awakening when I realised the extent of my unconscious assumptions and actions, all because society had ingrained the idea that "men don't show emotions" in me.

Once I became conscious of my behaviour, I couldn't unsee it. I noticed how I consistently made assumptions about men, thinking they lived and behaved strictly according to society's stereotypes. Conversations with some of my closest girlfriends revealed they had experienced a similar awakening and felt remorse for their past behaviours.

Stop and think for yourself. What are the things that come up for you when you think of "a woman" or "a man"? Whatever comes up, stupid or not (most likely as ridiculous as my assumptions), reflects how you unconsciously expect them to behave.

Letting Go of Our Assumptions That Live in Our Gender Boxes

Gender should never define authenticity or vulnerability. As leaders breaking free from those gender confines, we must create spaces where everyone can be genuine, irrespective of societal norms. It's about dismantling the idea that men should suppress their feelings and encouraging them to enter the vulnerable zone.

A radiant example of vulnerability's transformative essence comes to light through the inspiring journey of my dear friend and fellow changemaker, Bev Hancock.

As the tapestry of the new leadership rules unfolds, Bev's story, shared during my research for this book on *The Change Makers Podcast*, stands as a testament to vulnerability's pivotal role in authentic leadership. In the enchanting landscapes of South Africa, Bev's narrative unfolds, portraying vulnerability not as a weakness but as a conduit for strength and connection.

Her candid account reveals a life-altering crossroads—a divorce and the challenge of raising her two young boys on her own. This unfamiliar terrain compelled Bev to step out of her predefined role as a minister's wife, a role that no longer confined her. Throughout this voyage, Bev's unwavering resilience blossomed. Her journey from introversion to empowerment is a beacon of hope for those navigating similar paths.

Bev's "magic circle," a network of unwavering support, offered her solace during the darkest moments. She tackled self-doubt head-on, breaking free from the constraints of a low self-image. I found her story magnificently underscores the concept that vulnerability, when embraced, shapes us into formidable beacons of authenticity and resilience.

Through her unique tale, Bev advocates for vulnerability's capacity to nurture growth and a profound sense of belonging. Bev's story intertwines seamlessly, showcasing vulnerability's essence, a powerful force propelling us towards leadership beyond gender, fostering genuine connections and trans-formative change.

That brings me to you, a leader beyond genders, steering the ship towards a safe harbour of authenticity, vulnerability, and strengths.

How do you foster an environment where vulnerability is cherished, not shamed?

1. **Firstly, it's about walking the talk.** You show your vulnerabilities—share your concerns and admit your mistakes—thus paving the way for others to do the same. Vulnerability radiates courage. It's not a sign of fragility.

2. **Secondly, you practice active listening with an empathetic heart.** When your team or a family member opens up, be the confidante who understands and supports them without judgement. Create a culture where authenticity is celebrated and vulnerability is met with compassion. This, my friend, is where bonds grow more robust and trust flourishes.

3. **Thirdly, let humour be your ally.** Remember, laughter is the universal language that breaks barriers. A well-timed joke can ease tension, making it easier for everyone to peel off their armour and reveal their true selves. Vulnerability doesn't always have to be serious; it can be shared with a chuckle.

So, as you lead your team or your family beyond the confines of gendered expectations, remind yourself of these three pillars: be the authentic role model, compassionate listener, and master of lightheartedness.

Embracing vulnerability isn't just about you; it's about creating an environment where everyone feels safe enough to show up authentically.

Embracing vulnerability is a dynamic and ongoing journey that requires courage and self-compassion. As leaders, we understand that exposure might not always come naturally, and there will be moments of discomfort along the way. It's essential to acknowledge that even the most authentic and resilient leaders have moments of uncertainty.

These moments don't diminish our strength but illuminate our humanity. Just as we guide others through challenges, we must extend the same empathy to ourselves.

Embracing vulnerability doesn't mean eliminating all traces of fear; instead, it means forging ahead despite those fears. It's a process of growth, a step-by-step evolution that transforms vulnerability into a wellspring of strength.

So, if you find yourself grappling with vulnerability's complexities, remember that you're on a path many have walked before. Your journey is unique, and it's okay to experience discomfort.

Each step you take towards vulnerability is a testament to your commitment to authentic leadership and unwavering dedication to growth.

Authentic Connection: The Heartbeat of Vulnerability

When we enter the realm of authenticity and vulnerability, something magical happens: authentic connections form. You know, when you feel you can be yourself with another person, that magical feeling of acceptance. Imagine having a genuine connection with yourself first and then being able to connect with other people from that same source.

Imagine a space where you can be yourself, not who you think you must be. It's like taking off heavy armour you didn't even realise you were wearing. In this space, conversations flow; naturally, ideas bloom, and trust deepens.

It feels like a breath of fresh air, a warm embrace that says, "You are accepted as you are." It's the environment that brings out the best in everyone, where collaboration flourishes and innovation thrives. As we constantly mirror each other, when you accept who you are, you will find it easier to take others where they are.

This is the power of authentic connection, and it's a treasure you, as a leader beyond genders, are uniquely positioned to cultivate.

CHAPTER 10

Challenging the Status Quo: Disrupting Gender Norms

Be the spark that disrupts the norms,
the voice that challenges the status quo,
and the heart that ignites a revolution of equality.
In a world hungry for change,
let your actions be the transformative ripples
that redefine what's possible.

We are in an electrifying chapter. We're not just challenging the status quo—we're flipping it upside down and shaking it for good measure. It's time to shatter the mould of outdated gender norms, and we're doing it with energy, inspiration, and a dash of humour that'll leave us ready to take on the world.

Get ready to be bold, audacious, and utterly unapologetic as we dive into the thrilling adventure of disrupting the norms that have held us back for far too long.

Embracing Equity: Connecting Through Diversity

Imagine sitting down with someone and seeing them not as strangers but as part of your family.

A far-out idea?

What if you could shift your perspective for a few minutes and imagine the person sitting in front of you on the train or waiting in the car at the intersection is indeed a member of your family?

What if you could?

Could you extend that time to thirty minutes a day, then extend that to an hour?

Embracing equity and connecting through diversity is not about forcing everyone into the same box but celebrating humanity's vibrant spectrum. We're talking about tossing aside the value systems that keep us boxed in and giving ourselves and others the space to shine in our authentic brilliance.

Where there is a will, there is a way.

What if we ditch the preconceptions and judgements and embrace the kaleidoscope of traits, skills, and backgrounds that make us who we are?

Challenging?

Well, ask yourself, "What if I could see people for who they are, not by my assumptions?"

What would it give you back being able to do just that? What would it mean to be seen and valued for who you are?

Empowering Both Genders for a Thriving Society: Fashioning a New Normal

Picture this: a world where clothing isn't a gender-based battleground. That's right; we're challenging the norms that dictate what men and women should wear. What if we could liberate fashion from the chains of traditional gender roles and set a new standard where self-expression is the only rule, ensuring everyone feels confident and free to strut their stuff, from dresses to suits, no matter what they wear. Because guess what? It's not just about the fabric; it's about the power of self-expression. And if this idea makes your stomach turn, ask yourself this: Is that dislike because you're not used to seeing men in dresses, or is it because you've only experienced men in dresses to be out of the norm? Whatever it is, just pay attention to your unconscious biases having a ball.

One "what if" question ignited a change in Australia, challenging the norms and redefining conversations.

At a conference in Australia, my blog post pondering the acceptance of boys wearing skirts and dresses was in the spotlight. The audience, composed of senior HR leaders in Australia's workplace, discussed health and wellness. While the notion of breaking away from gender norms garnered resistance from most, one brave soul dared question, "Well, why not?"

The conference room atmosphere grew charged in moments as this courageous voice spoke up, daring to introduce a different narrative.

The aftermath of that query was swift and surprising. The person who raised their voice in favour of breaking gender stereotypes found themselves escorted out of the room by security guards.

Why?

Because they were courageous enough to ask a question for a new conversation outside societal norms. Their simple question was a plea for exploration and expansion beyond the rigid boundaries we often accept.

This individual wasn't advocating that all boys should wear dresses. Instead, they were advocating for **choice, just as girls have.** They were ready to learn to comprehend a perspective that deviates from the norm. Like the child in the "Emperor's New Clothes" tale or Aristotle challenging the flat Earth belief, this individual dared to see differently and question the status quo.

Amidst the pressures to conform to pre-established gender roles, this act of courage stands as a beacon. The fear of societal backlash often forces us into roles and behaviours that don't align with our true selves, leading to unhappiness and even mental health struggles. The way forward is by fostering a willingness to learn and question. This is the foundation for actual change. And to that end, embracing curiosity is vital.

By being the change, by allowing ourselves to be open and authentic, we create a ripple effect. We grant permission to others to shed their masks and be genuine too. It's a path to individual and collective growth, where societal constructs are dismantled, and the space for evolution is embraced.

Who that courageous woman at the conference was remains a mystery to me, but her audacity is a gift that keeps giving. We must remind ourselves that societal norms are subject to evolution and change.

Acceptance in one society may differ in another. Our role as individuals is to be open to learning, understanding, and forging bridges towards progress. Imagine the power of such a shift, allowing those around us to survive and thrive simply by being their authentic selves.

The journey to a better tomorrow can start with the courage to ask "Why not?" and the openness to pursue the answers.

Admitting to your 188 biases is a strength!

Hold on to your hats, folks, because it's time to face the truth: biases are as common as the air we breathe.

But here's the thing. Admitting them is not a weakness; it's a strength. It's about recognising that we all have room to grow, learn, and expand our perspectives.

We're debunking the myth that certain biases are inherent and doing it with gusto.

Say goodbye to stereotypes that limit our awareness and potential and hello to a world where we see people for who they indeed are, not what society has labelled them to be.

Unconscious Biases Can Affect Anyone, Regardless of Gender

The world has been more focused on pointing out the many bias's women get. For example, the UN gave a report earlier this year (2023) indicating that 90 percent of humanity holds biases against women. That means both men and women hold biases against women!

Fact bomb! Our world is very occupied with biases against women, and rightfully so. However, I have not seen any report about the damage of our prejudices against men. Have you?

Can we have this critical conversation about biases against women without simultaneously looking at our prejudgements against men? Well, what if we have conversations about our prejudices against all genders? Open for a deeper discussion without pointing fingers to blame someone else.

Let's look at ten common unconscious biases some women hold against men.

1. **Emotional Expression:** Assuming that men should be less emotional or stoic, disregarding their feelings or struggles as less valid.

2. **Competence Doubt:** Believing that men are less competent in traditionally feminine roles such as cooking, caregiving, or emotional support.

3. **Lack of Nurturing Abilities:** Assuming that men are less nurturing or incapable of caring for children or family members.

4. **Leadership Stereotypes:** Believing that men are inherently more suited for leadership positions, dismissing their qualifications or skills.

5. **Involvement in Child-Rearing:** Assuming that men are less involved in childcare or household responsibilities, perpetuating gender roles.

6. **Lack of Empathy:** Presuming that men are less empathetic or understanding, overlooking their capacity to offer emotional support.

7. **Communication Styles:** Believing that men are less effective communicators, ignoring their ability to engage in meaningful conversations.

8. **Appearance and Self-Care:** Assuming men are less concerned about their appearance or self-care, disregarding their grooming and well-being.

9. **Interest in Arts and Humanities:** Believing that men are less interested in arts, humanities, or creative pursuits, limiting their self-expression.

10. **Physical Abilities:** Assuming that men are naturally more physically capable, discounting their emotions or vulnerabilities.

Pay very close attention to your reactions to this list, especially when you find yourself agreeing with one or more of these assumptions. Your responses say a lot about how you treat other men around you and your assumptions about men.

Men are not loving, kind, and caring. Is that true?

Let me share a profound experience from a conference that delved into the intricate realm of gender stereotypes. During one eye-opening exercise, participants were divided into workgroups tasked with jotting down words that spontaneously came to mind when thinking about "men" and "women."

The general stereotypes became glaringly evident as the ink flowed and words filled the A2 papers. The paper for men was adorned with descriptors like forceful, strong, leaders, and verbal, while the sheets about women bore words like beauty, softness, and kindness. It was a stark reminder of how these ingrained stereotypes are verbally manifested repeatedly, shaping our perceptions.

During this exercise, a personal revelation struck me. I asked myself, "What genuinely comes to mind when I think of men?" The answer emerged as clear as day: **loving, caring, kind**.

I courageously shared these words with the group's leader, who promptly recorded them on the paper. However, what followed was a poignant moment that highlighted the power of individual experiences. A woman from East Europe, her tone tinged with anger, protested vehemently, asserting, "Men are not loving, caring, and kind." She insisted that my words be erased from the A2 sheet.

This exchange struck a chord with me. It begged the question: could her life experiences have led her to believe that loving, caring, and kind men were impossible? And if she had sons, grandsons, or a loving partner, did this steadfast belief inadvertently close her to the possibility of experiencing these beautiful qualities from the men in her life? It was a heart-wrenching reminder of how entrenched judgements can skew our perceptions, limiting our capacity to see beyond preconceived notions and embrace the full spectrum of human potential, regardless of gender.

The Difference Between Believing in Something and the Actual Truth

It's essential to recognise that these biases are harmful and counterproductive.

Challenging and addressing unconscious biases benefits everyone by fostering a more inclusive and understanding society.

Let's look a bit deeper.

Unconscious Biases Exist in Both Women and Men

Here are ten common unconscious biases that individuals have—five of them regardless of gender and another five held only against women, by women. Yes, you read that correctly. Both men and women have these biases against women!

Biases Held by Both Women and Men:

1. **Leadership Abilities:** Assuming that women are less capable of leadership, even when they possess the necessary skills and experience.

2. **Emotional Decision-Making:** Believing women make decisions based on emotions rather than rational thinking.

3. **Caregiver Roles:** Presuming women are more suitable for caregiving roles, overlooking their expertise in other areas.

4. **Technical Skills:** Assuming that women are less proficient in specialised fields, discounting their abilities in STEM (science, technology, engineering, mathematics).

5. **Ambition and Career Focus:** Believing that women should be more focused on their careers and ambition despite their determination and drive.

Biases More Commonly Held Against Women by Women:

1. **Appearance Bias:** Evaluating women based on appearance rather than their skills or contributions.

2. **Motherhood Assumptions:** Assuming that women with children are less committed to their careers or are more distracted.

3. **Communication Styles:** Perceiving assertive women as aggressive, while assertive men are considered confident.

4. **Competence Doubt:** Believing that women must prove themselves more than men in professional settings.

5. **Negotiation Skills:** Assuming that women are less effective negotiators, which affects their advancement in salary and promotions.

Acknowledging and confronting these biases is crucial to creating a more equitable and inclusive society.

When you notice you just made an assumption, you can always correct yourself and blame it on the box, saying, "Oh, I'm sorry, I think I just put you into a box," or when you feel someone is making assumptions about you, you can also gently say, "I think you just put me into a box that I don't belong in."

By challenging these assumptions, we can ensure that women have equal opportunities and are evaluated based on their skills, expertise, and contributions.

Equal Pay, Equal Opportunities: Unleashing the Power of the Purse

Let's talk about the elephant in the room: money. We've been stuck in a narrative where gender dictates our relationship with finances, and its high time we break free.

Women are not "bad" with money, and men don't have some secret financial superpower.

You and I know that generalising 50 percent of the human population this way is false!

Some women might have been raised believing that money and finances weren't something their beautiful little heads should consider.

Can you see how ridiculous a statement this is?

Well, it is absurd because it's just a made-up concept! The consequence of believing that because you are a woman you are not supposed to be interested in or even have the capacity to work with money is simply a made-up box!

Before you jump up in your seat and want to point at someone who influenced this belief in your life, stop and think more about what you will do to change that narrative. That action step will impact the rest of your life, not pointing fingers at someone from the past who might have said something or told you something that influenced you till this day.

The Dire Consequences of Surrendering Our Strengths to Societal Norms

Take my friend Beth (not her real name) for instance. With a knack for money and investments, she triumphed with a vast real estate portfolio. In her late thirties, she married a finance man. Despite her proven capability of handling her money and influenced by the narrative that women should receive, and men should lead, she handed her finances over to him. As their marriage ended, so did the illusion of her husband's financial prowess. In the wake of their economic turmoil, Beth is embittered by the outcome, blaming the patriarchal system, not her own blindness, for her giving away her strength.

Instead of embracing the perspective that life unfolds for her—"Life happens for you," as my friend Gido mentioned— she sees herself as a victim. And it's heartbreaking to see her struggles. This story exemplifies the pitfalls of yielding to societal norms rather than harnessing one's inherent strengths.

Beth's tale makes me wonder how different her path might have been if she'd let her unique financial prowess shine, challenged the norm, and shunned the gendered expectations imposed by society.

As a leader who leads beyond gender, you take responsibility and work on the person you want to become. And it could be a financial wizard per excellence.

The same self-leadership approach goes for any man who's been told he should be responsible for the home's finances because "that's what men are supposed to do." He could be inept at handling finances for the family, perhaps even as meaningless as his father and his grandfather were. Yet, he's mindlessly following the socially constructed gender role, stuck in that box, and trying to hide his futile approach to money.

To any man or woman who wants to improve their relationship with money and finances, I only have one thing to say. If you want to improve your relationship with money and finances, there is only one way forward. Take responsibility, work on it, and start today!

The profound wisdom I received from my friend Loa says it all: "There is only one thing certain about your partner or spouse in life. They will eventually leave you; they will either die or leave, so you better have your finances in order." —Thordís Lóa Thorhallsdóttir

It's time to level the playing field and let skills, dedication, and hard work determine our financial worth. Whether it's investments, savings, or budgeting, let's dance to our own financial tune and create a world where equal pay, and genderless interest and access to finance, isn't just a dream— it's the reality we deserve.

Playing the Sport and Honouring the Hobby They Love: Erasing the Lines

Sports and hobbies are passions that should know no gender boundaries. We're smashing the notion that certain activities are meant for one gender or another. It's time to celebrate talent, skill, and dedication, regardless of who's displaying it.

From football fields to basketball courts, let's transform the battle of the sexes into a celebration of a shared love for the game. Whether it's a soccer jersey or a ballet tutu, let's embrace a world where everyone can pursue their passions unburdened by stereotypes.

Equality should go for sports just as in other life aspects.

Today, women's sports are far from being valued the same way as men's. And gosh, the media could get their ducks in a row in this area. Have you seen the questions women in sports get from the press versus men? It's stereotyping, as if the folks working in the media have swallowed *Mad Men* episodes with their breakfast daily.

When the day comes that the press asks men how they manage to be in sports and running a family simultaneously, we might have gotten one step further. So far, I am still waiting to see an interview who asks men those types of questions to the same extent women are asked.

Open Communication and Emotional Expression: Unleashing the Spectrum

Get ready for a roller coaster of emotions! We're tackling the idea that certain feelings belong to specific genders.

What if we ditch that "masculine" and "feminine" emotional boxing match once and for all and let emotions flow freely? Anger, vulnerability, strength, and compassion are all part of the beautiful spectrum of human emotions. Why label them by gender stereotype?

We can create a world where communication soars, empathy flourishes, and vulnerability is seen as a strength, not a weakness.

We can break down those emotional walls and build bridges of understanding.

Continuous Personal Growth: The Adventure of a Lifetime

Guess what, folks? Personal growth is not a one-gender game. It's a universal banquet of wisdom, and everyone is invited. And here is an encouragement to some men out there (you know if I'm talking to you): it's time to pull up a chair and feast on the endless opportunities for self-improvement. It's your life. Give yourself the gift of unleashing yourself from the social constructs that have been placed on you.

You can kick the outdated stereotypes to the curb and embrace the joy of learning, the excitement of growth, and the empowerment of self-improvement. Level up, gain new skills, and explore the uncharted territories of your potential.

Personal development isn't just about changing; it's about becoming the best version of yourself. So, why wait? Let's dive into the adventure of personal growth hand in hand.

Being Role Models and Challenging Unconscious Bias: Sparking the Ripple Effect

Picture a world where each of us embodies the qualities of a role model. Hang on a minute! You don't have to imagine. That's the fact. You are a role model. Your actions, reactions, and view of the world matter and influence others around you.

It's about being aware of our actions, reactions, and judgements and using that awareness to challenge unconscious biases.

By embodying this mindset, we become catalysts for positive change, inspiring others to follow suit. It's a ripple effect transforming society into a haven of inclusivity and equity.

Empathy, Collaboration, and Active Listening in Leadership: The Recipe for Success

Leadership, regardless of gender, shines brightest when empathy, collaboration, and active listening are its foundation.

It's about understanding and addressing the needs of our teams, fostering innovation, and celebrating diverse perspectives. Let's be leaders who create harmonious and supportive work environments where every voice is valued and heard.

It's time to cultivate a leadership style that embraces the power of unity.

Being Brave and Speaking Up: A Call to Action

It's time to amplify our voices and advocate for ourselves and others. By being brave and speaking up, we set the stage for a culture of empowerment and accountability.

This isn't about men or women; it's about humanity coming together to create a world where every voice matters.

So, let's join hands and rewrite the narrative where equality isn't just a dream; it's a reality we're creating every day.

Creating Actionable Strategies Towards an Equitable Future

In pursuing challenging and disrupting gender norms, we must equip ourselves with actionable strategies that propel us towards an equitable future.

One practical step is to engage in open conversations with friends, family, and colleagues about the limitations of gender stereotypes. Doing it in a light, humorous way is a good strategy as this topic is, for some, an issue they are getting tired of visiting.

Sharing personal experiences and encouraging others to do the same can foster understanding and empathy. For instance, openly discussing how diverse interests and hobbies defy traditional gender boundaries can create a ripple effect of awareness.

Another empowering approach is actively seeking and supporting media, art, and literature that portrays diverse gender roles and identities. By consciously choosing content that challenges norms, we contribute to reshaping cultural narratives.

Additionally, championing equal opportunities and shared responsibilities in professional and personal settings can inspire change.

Encouraging colleagues to recognise and address unconscious biases in decision-making processes can lead to more inclusive work environments. Moreover, participating in or organising workshops and seminars on gender awareness can educate and influence larger communities.

By initiating these dialogues and actions, we can collectively dismantle outdated gender norms and forge an inclusive path forward.

Embracing Equality: A Journey of Empowerment

As we wrap up this chapter, remember this: embracing equality and challenging gender norms isn't just a revolutionary act; it's a journey of empowerment. It's about rewriting the narrative for generations to come. It's about valuing every individual's unique contribution and creating a world where diversity is celebrated.

So, let's step boldly into this future where men and women lead beyond gender, enriching lives, fostering collaboration, and inspiring an inclusive, thriving, unstoppable world.

Forging Keys to Unlock Boundless Potential

In the grand tapestry of humanity, we are the threads of change, the weavers of a new narrative. As we close the door on this chapter, remember that disrupting gender norms isn't just about breaking chains—it's about forging keys to unlock boundless potential.

We've ignited a revolution of possibilities, and with every step we take, every conversation we start, every bias we challenge, we're shaping a world where equality is the heartbeat of society.

Let us continue to lead beyond gender to inspire, uplift, and create a legacy of inclusivity and empowerment. The future we're building is one where diversity thrives, voices are heard, and everyone who desires can spread their wings and soar.

Our journey is far from over. It's a harmony of courage, a dance of determination, and a chorus of hope. As we embrace equality with open hearts, we craft a world where all dreams are possible. Onward, champions of change, as we write the next chapter of a revolution that echoes through time.

CHAPTER 11

Unmasking the Gender Tango: Navigating Identity and Preconceived Roles

It's a curious dance we find ourselves in, one that's been choreographed for generations, where household chores and gender roles perform a complex tango.

The gender box is full of preconceived gender roles regardless of who we are or what makes our hearts sing joyfully.

In Iceland, a country that has held the top rank for gender equality for fourteen consecutive years, these choreographed gender roles still cling to our society. I said it before, and I will repeat it again: "Just because we have ranked number one worldwide for gender equality doesn't mean we've got it. It only means we are not as bad as the other nations!"

The recent Gallup Poll in Iceland unveiled a peculiar dance that we haven't quite mastered the steps to. Even with today's machinery that no longer requires sheer physical strength, we still expect men to take on specific roles and women others. It's as if we're dancing to a tune written in the past, one that refuses to evolve with the times.

According to the study, Icelandic women care for the third-shift part of the household, meaning the many unspoken mental responsibilities, remembering Aunt Alma's birthday and little Joe's doctors' appointments, much more than their male partners, but men perceive the division of labour as more equal than women. In other words, women "feel" like they do much more household chores, but men see that they share things equally with their female partners.

Isn't that interesting?

This is revealed in the same National Gallup poll on the division of household chores in Iceland.

When women in heterosexual relationships were asked how household chores were divided between them and their spouses, 67 percent said they did more of them. In contrast, 12 percent of men said they did more household chores. Half of the men said their spouse did more, and 6 percent of women said their spouse did more.

There are some differences in household chores men and women take care of at home. Women are more likely to dry and clean the bathroom; buy gifts, clothes, and furniture; load the dishwasher; vacuum; change sheets; and grocery shop. On the other hand, men are more likely to take out the trash, mow the lawn, take the car for repairs, and handle home repairs.

Dishwashing is the household chore that is most equally divided between the genders.

It's also interesting to see that many of the men's chores don't have to be done daily.

You don't mow the lawn or take the car for daily repairs, right? But loading the dishwasher or grocery shopping is a daily chore.

So, according to this study, it looks like people in heterosexual relationships experience things quite differently.

I've asked myself: Are women generally taking on these roles because they see it as part of their identity? Their script, the program constantly running in their system, has convinced them that this is who they are—a caregiver. Not by their choice but by the rules the society has made them believe they have to accept. This leaves them with one more "I should" or "I have to," not because they love it so much, but more because that's what they see as their role because they are women and that is what their mother and grandmother did back in their days.

I've also asked myself: How many couples talk openly about how they want to divide household chores, inducing the third watch? Do you know many couples who have had a deep conversation before they went into marriage or a partnership about which partner would do what, such as plan and remember birthdays, doctors' appointments, visit Grandma, etc? To consciously choose how they want to live their lives from who they authentically are?

I don't know any. I know plenty of people, mostly women, who have moaned or complained about their partner not doing one thing or another in the household. But I can't recall people having deep conversations, including making personal commitments, about who will do what of these hidden tasks on the third shift.

Example: As an example of a common third-shift task, is it essential for all couples to celebrate all birthdays in the family? If so, choose who takes responsibility for it based on who loves doing that task rather than assuming it will be done by the gender that society has placed that role upon.

Because we constantly make assumptions, these conversations most likely don't exist. Therefore, it's more likely that you take on the gender role you saw your mother or grandmother or other females in your family or father or grandfather or other males in your family assume.

But just because that's what you've done in the past doesn't mean you have to do it in the present or future.

Your identity isn't static unless you make it such; it can easily be fluid.

These gender roles often become a part of our identity, entwined so profoundly within us that they are difficult to untangle. They shape not just what we do but also how we perceive ourselves.

For years, I saw myself as a "doer." I was always busy doing something, believing that's what defined me. It was a big part of my identity. Little did I realise that I was constantly on the run, neglecting the essence of simply being a "human being." Noticing my behaviour made me rethink who I wanted to be . . . and also allowed me to ask myself a more profound question: Who do I want to become?

You are not the person you were a year ago or a decade ago.

There was another identity I held on to for decades, one that seemed trivial but was rather revealing. I had convinced myself and everyone around me that I was a terrible baker. This identity took root, and I repeatedly said, "I'm a terrible baker." As if I was afraid of being asked to be in a baking challenge, I made it clear to everyone that I was not a baker.

Then, one day, I admired a friend who always brings these delicious homemade cakes to events and parties. I just envied her for her skills, passion, and the wonderful feeling she brought to these events. It made me ponder: Why do I keep telling this story that I'm a terrible baker? What am I seeking in people's reactions when I say this? Is it part of my rebellion against gender stereotypes?

At the same time, I realised that I wished to be the person who arrives at a gathering with a homemade cake or something delightful. That realisation prompted me to challenge my narrative, embark on a baking adventure, and transform my story. And I set out to learn how to bake.

I changed my story from being the "terrible baker" to the story "you know I always bring cakes with me" (I even said that the first time I brought a homemade cake with me). We can change our identity by changing our behaviours and stories.

Are traditional gender roles here to stay? What if we could change them without being judged or labelled as being a "feminine man" or people being convinced you are "gay" because you love to think about and arrange decorations for your home or parties? Or that you are a "tomboy" if you are an unapologetic woman, straightforward, or love cars, motorbikes, or a web of cables and electronics?

These humorous role reversals illuminate the absurdity of gender-defined responsibilities in our modern world, shedding light on the inherent biases that persist beneath the surface.

Now, let's break down these stereotypes and create a road map for leaders ready to embrace the new rules of leadership beyond gender.

The Third Watch: The Covert Timekeeper Draining Your Time and Energy

Now, let's examine the "third watch" a bit further. This term, often unseen and unspoken, encompasses the countless responsibilities we take on without notice.

I hear more and more women around me who have had incredible careers that burn out because they are working in a high-level job and doing a big chunk of this so-called third watch, giving them hardly any time to breathe, let alone play a round of golf or video games like so many of my male friends seem to find time to do.

In my life, the division of labour regarding family birthdays is a prime example. My partner and I navigate the intricate web of our extended families. I take care of my part of the family, and he takes responsibility for his part of the family. On the surface, it's a seemingly trivial task, but beneath lies a tapestry of expectations and societal norms.

People celebrate Óli, my partner, with great admiration when he takes on a task that society sees as a woman's role, but they don't say a thing when I do the same thing. Sound familiar to you?

Using AI and Technology to Help Us Create Space for Open Conversations

I want my home to be clean and tidy, but my partner, is . . . well, let's say a bit less keen. I didn't want him to get away with not cleaning, so I, like many of my soul sisters, grew weary of constantly asking him to vacuum. Let's make one thing clear. One of the identities I do not want to hold is the nagging woman. I would rather do the job myself than be the person who is constantly nagging.

The solution? I suggested we would buy a vacuum robot. At first, my partner wasn't too sure about it. It only took me one sentence to change his uncertainty about purchasing this equipment to action.

I simply said: *"Óli minn* (Icelandic meaning "My dear Óli"), imagine never hearing me again asking you to vacuum the floor." He looked at me, and his face lit up with excitement.

The decision to buy a vacuum robot was on the table. Today, we have a trusty companion I affectionately named Alfred. In today's world, such equipment can play a pivotal role in breaking free from traditional gender choreography.

But the real key lies in self-awareness and communication. It's about recognising when we perform tasks out of habit and ritual, often driven by unconscious gender roles.

The power of sitting down at the table, not to nag but to engage in a thoughtful discussion about what truly matters to us as a family, a couple, or a unity, cannot be underestimated.

Action Points and Reflection:

- Reflect on your experiences with gender-defined chores and roles. Have you ever felt confined by these stereotypes?

- Consider how these stereotypes might have shaped your identity. Are there roles you've adopted as a part of who you are?

- Challenge yourself to break free from these unconscious programs. Identify one chore or responsibility you can shift or share with others based on passion and skill rather than gender.

- Initiate an open conversation with your family or team about collectively challenging traditional assignments and embracing a more inclusive and holistic approach to leadership and household responsibilities.

CHAPTER 12

The Ripple Effect:
Inspiring Change Beyond Ourselves

"When we challenge our thoughts,
we unleash the power of conscious awareness.
Free yourself from the limitations of conditioned thinking."
—Gido Schimanski.

Hey, there. Let's talk about being leaders who rock the boat in the best way possible! You know, our actions aren't just one-time events. They're more like throwing a stone into a pond and watching the ripples go wild. Imagine those ripples as the impact of our leadership, making waves that reach far and wide beyond what we can see.

We have incredible power to make things happen. I'm talking about inspiring change, getting others on board, and creating a chain reaction of transformation that sweeps through the world.

Building a ripple effect starts with one pebble at a time. Throughout history, big game changers have cleared the path, fighting for people's rights to be seen, valued, and respected as they are.

The Game Changers: LGBTQ+ and women's rights movements are shaping leadership beyond gender right now. Change is happening all around us. The LGBTQ+ and the women's rights movement's brushstrokes have created waves beyond their own stories.

The LGBTQ+ movement is about being accepted and loved for who you are. Their journey has a significant impact, shaking up the idea of strict gender roles. They're teaching us that love is love, no matter what. And this isn't just about them; it's changing how we all think about love, respect, and equality.

Then we've got the women's rights movement breaking down old-fashioned ideas about what women can or can't do. This isn't just about gender; it's about showing that everyone, regardless of gender, can be a leader.

The cool thing is these two movements work together to create a new way of thinking. They're showing us that the old rules about gender don't fit anymore. People realise that love and leadership don't have to work in a box.

This shift is making a big difference in how we see ourselves and others, and it's helping us move towards leadership that's not about gender.

So, what does this mean for all of us?

Everyone's Empowered: The LGBTQ+ and women's rights movements give people the confidence to stand up, be themselves, and lead. As these movements gain momentum, more people from all walks of life say, "Hey, I can do this too!"

Language Upgrade: With old gender norms being tossed out, our words and stories are changing too. We're telling stories that include everyone, and this helps us understand each other better.

Embracing Our Differences: The movements remind us that people aren't just one thing. We're all a mix of different parts: our gender, race, and background. By celebrating these differences, we make the world a more exciting and inclusive place.

Listening to our deepest desires is more important than following what society tells us each time.

In *The Change Makers Podcast—Leadership Beyond Gender* series, episode #148, I interviewed the magical Neerja Singh.

Neerja Singh shares a profoundly moving and poignant story that speaks to the immense power of our actions and their far-reaching consequences. Neerja's daughter, who tragically ended her life due to the suffocating weight of societal expectations, delivers a heartbreaking reminder of the urgent need for change. In Neerja's final conversation, her daughter's poignant words echo with profound truth: "I never wanted career success; all I ever wanted was to be a mum."

Her story reminds us that despite all the empowerment and focus on women's education and valuable input into the business world, it doesn't mean that ALL women want to place their success in the outside world. Some deeply desire to be mothers full-time. And that should be fine!

Neerja's narrative is a stark testament to the devastating impact of societal norms and the pressing need to dismantle them. As we delve into the essence of inspiring change beyond ourselves, Neerja's story ignites a call to action.

It emphasises the importance of creating an environment where we listen, where individuals are free from the constraints of harmful expectations, and where they can truly flourish as their authentic selves.

Neerja's courage to share her daughter's experience inspires us to work towards a more compassionate and inclusive world where every individual's dreams are cherished, and their true essence is valued.

Through her story, Neerja shows us how even the smallest of actions can create ripples of transformation that extend far beyond ourselves, touching the lives of countless others.

Put all this together, and it's like the start of a new leadership era. One where being true to yourself, being kind, and understanding others matters.

As the lines between gender roles blur, we enter a new world. It is a world where leadership isn't just for some people but for everyone.

We're becoming part of creating change, making things more equal, and building a world where everyone belongs.

Be the Change, and Watch the Ripples Spread

There are so many inspirational stories of people creating ripples of change. Let's look at some who've made a considerable impact.

Heard of Malala Yousafzai? She's all about girls' education and empowerment. Then there's Mahatma Gandhi, who believed in peaceful change and made a big difference.

Let those stories of people who have created ripple effects of change around them inspire you to do the same. If you don't already have stories of your own about your ripple effect, it only means two things: either you have not seen the impact you've had on people, or you are about to become the change you want to see in your world. Be careful not to think you must be famous for making change happen. Just stand up for what you believe in, for yourself and others.

Dealing with Doubts

If you're not feeling like a world-changer, it might be because you're underestimating your power. We're talking about those sneaky thoughts that hold you back—the ones that say you're not good enough or things must be perfect.

Ahh . . . yeah, those thoughts, you might be saying to yourself and nodding.

They're like a made-up story that's keeping you from making waves.

Here's a tip from Gido Schimanski, my wonderful friend and fellow changemaker from *The Change Makers Podcast—Leadership Beyond Gender*, episode number 146, "The Ripple Effect: Changing Inner Worlds, Transforming the Environment."

Gido points out, "Don't believe everything you think . . . Step outside and see the situation from a new angle."

It's like seeing things clearly and not falling for your mind's tricks. In a world where thoughts are like a bunch of fireflies dancing around, Gido's advice is golden.

Give your thoughts a side-eye, ask them tough questions, and figure out if they're real or just telling stories.

Taking Steps to Create a Ripple of Change Takes Bravery

It's like deciding to wear your favourite funky socks to a fancy party. You're being bold, you're standing out, and you're making a statement.

Here's the secret sauce: vulnerability and authenticity. These two things make your ripple of change even more powerful. It's like dancing your heart out at a party, not caring how goofy you look.

Delving Deeper into the Ripple Effect

As we delve deeper into the ripple-effect concept, we uncover a profound truth: its transformative power extends beyond mere change propagation. It's a force that resonates deeply with our mission of dismantling restrictive gender norms and fostering inclusive leadership. Just as a stone thrown into a pond sends ripples in all directions, our actions as leaders can disrupt the stagnant waters of traditional gender roles.

Each ripple represents an act of defiance against the limitations imposed by societal expectations. As these ripples spread, they convey that leadership isn't confined by gender. Our commitment to inclusive leadership catalyses a wave of understanding transcending the binary notion of leadership roles. It's a clarion call to lead beyond predetermined boundaries and embrace the full spectrum of human potential, irrespective of gender.

By creating this ripple effect, we champion a new era of leadership where diversity thrives, and every voice has a chance to make waves.

So, let's sum it up with a few core takeaways to help you create ripple effects around you as a leader who leads beyond gender.

Play with Your Thoughts: Have fun challenging your thoughts and questioning their truth.

Unlearn Old Ideas: Get rid of old beliefs that limit and stop you from being yourself.

Brave Moves: Be courageous enough to challenge the norm and make a change.

Be Real: Embrace being vulnerable and authentic to yourself; it's like your secret weapon.

Start a Ripple: Remember, your actions can set off a chain reaction of change that reaches far beyond your circle.

Add some self-reflection time:

- How often do those sneaky and limiting thoughts hold you back?

- How can you give them a run for their money?

- What's something you'd like to change?

- How can you be brave and make it happen?

- How can being authentic and showing vulnerability make you a better leader?

- Are you ready to start your own ripple of change, making the world better?

"When we question our thoughts, we unlock our conscious superpower. Break free from those old ways of thinking." — Gido Schimanski

Sir John Whitmore's research was a punch in the stomach!

In the vibrant tapestry of leadership, let's look at the heart of transformation—fostering inclusive environments and cultivating the hallowed ground of belonging.

As we journey through the realms of wisdom, let us pause and draw inspiration from the luminous teachings I was so lucky to receive from Sir John Whitmore, the distinguished author of *Coaching for Performance* and a heralded leadership coach.

I took part in gathering a group of senior leaders, their minds brimming with knowledge, skills, and potential, summoned by Sir John in Iceland. In this unique leadership workshop, he posed a simple yet profound question: How much of your precious capacities do you honestly use daily?

An exercise of collective introspection followed, revealing an astonishing truth: an average of merely 20 percent was being harnessed. Think about it . . . only 20 percent.

This revelation, resonating across continents, was an epiphany that awakened the spirit of transformation.

With a twinkle in his eye, Sir John ignited a spark of possibility by asking, "What if you could increase this by just two or three points? Or even by five to ten points?"

This result opened my eyes to how we are constantly limiting ourselves, and as I've shared earlier, his words also made me think about how we are wasting human resources this way.

What is stopping us from using more than 20 percent of our capabilities? you might be asking yourself.

At the core, the internal stop sign we are operating from prevents us from moving forward.

- **Clarity**—We need to figure out where we are going or what we want.

- **Confidence**—Mindsets are cluttered and filled with unconscious and conscious doubts about our ability to succeed.

- **We are all conditioned** by our society, upbringing, the people we surround ourselves with, etc. Women are often prepared to believe it's not ladylike to stand up and speak your way. It's not feminine, for example, or all the men who have been and are on company boards who don't stand up and do a thing because they are conditioned to believe it's not their place unless they are the chair of the committee as an example.

Whatever your reason is for not stepping up your game, let Sir John's observation sink in. Let it resonate deeply. Envision the life you could live, the impact you could make if you dared to be more of yourself.

With the wisdom of Sir John as our guiding star, let's step onto the dance floor of change, boldly embracing our potential, and co-created a world where each voice shines with the brilliance it deserves.

As we conclude chapter 12, let us embrace the profound truth that leadership beyond gender isn't a black-or-white concept but a vibrant spectrum of possibility. Neerja Singh's poignant story reminds us that our actions, no matter how seemingly small, have the potential to create ripples of change that transcend gender and touch the very core of humanity.

Each of us holds the power to challenge norms, shatter expectations, and inspire the world around us. In this intricate tapestry of leadership, let us remember that true empowerment lies in breaking free from confines, embracing our unique journeys, and nurturing an environment where everyone's dreams and aspirations can flourish.

As we move forward, let's carry Neerja's daughter's heartfelt wish—a longing for motherhood, not career glory—as a beacon of inspiration, driving us to cultivate a society that empowers individuals to chase their true passions, regardless of gender.

Next time you hear someone express their deepest desires, listen carefully, and allow them to talk about it even further— without giving them your view. After all, it's their desires, not yours!

In this world painted with the vibrant hues of diversity, may our shared efforts manifest the colours of change and progress, weaving a tapestry of leadership beyond gender that reflects the brilliance of each individual.

Remember, your journey to leadership beyond gender goes beyond just you. It's a symphony of influence, a dance of change. That's why we're all together, creating ripples that touch lives and shape a world of equality and togetherness.

So, let's get out there and make those ripples count!

CHAPTER 13

Unleashing the Creativity Within: Igniting Innovation

Creativity knows no gender boundaries. In this chapter, we'll tap into the wellspring of creativity. We'll ignite innovation, nurture out-of-the-box thinking, and foster a culture of creativity in our leadership endeavours. Get ready to unleash your imagination, my friend, for it is through creativity that we shape the world and open doors to endless possibilities.

In the tapestry of the new leadership rules beyond genders, we often find that the most profound stories arise from the deepest wells of personal experience.

A shining example is the journey of the change-maker, bestselling author, and transformational leader Susanne Frandsen, a beacon of transformation and innovation.

In my *Change Makers Podcast* interview with Susanne, she shared the shadows of a challenging upbringing. Susanne emerged not as a victim but as a victor of her circumstances. Her story embodies the essence of chapter 13, where we'll delve into the wellspring of creativity and the courage to embrace change.

Growing up in an environment where love seemed scarce and acceptance even more inadequate, Susanne's early years could have dictated her fate. Yet, against the odds, she chose a different path. Instead of harbouring bitterness, Susanne drew strength from her experiences, and through sheer determination, she transcended the constraints that life tried to impose upon her. Academically and professionally, she soared, an example of how adversity can become a catalyst for brilliance.

But Susanne's journey wasn't just about academic achievements or professional success. It was a voyage of self-discovery, learning to peel away layers of self-imposed limitations and societal expectations. Her multiple divorces, far from being seen as failures, became stepping-stones on her path to self-acceptance and authenticity. When she chose to break free from the corporate world and venture into entrepreneurship, she illuminated a paradigm shift that resonates with the essence of this chapter.

Susanne's story tells us that creativity is born from success and the willingness to embrace change and remain open to new possibilities. Her ability to say "yes" to opportunities, even when they seemed daunting, is a testament to the transformative power of self-belief and resilience.

Susanne's advocacy for feeling and processing emotions reveals a profound truth: that authenticity and vulnerability are the wellsprings of innovation in a world that often compartmentalises emotions away from professional spaces.

As we delve into chapter 13, let's allow Susanne Frandsen's journey inspire us.

Let us recognise that our past need not define us but can be the foundation upon which we build a future brimming with creativity, innovation, and the unwavering courage to say "yes" to change.

Susanne Frandsen's journey is a testament to the profound link between her path of personal transformation and the promotion of creativity and innovation within the realm of leadership beyond gender.

Her experiences, marked by overcoming adversity and transcending societal constraints, beautifully mirror the challenges that have historically limited individuals from diverse gender backgrounds in their leadership potential. Susanne's refusal to be confined by gender norms allowed her to break free from the limitations imposed upon her, illustrating the power of authenticity and self-belief. By embracing her unique journey and cultivating a culture of inclusivity and acceptance, Susanne not only shattered the glass ceiling that often stifles creativity but also catalysed an environment where diverse perspectives thrive.

Her story showcases that leadership beyond gender necessitates dismantling stereotypes and fostering an atmosphere where every individual's potential can flourish. In embracing her true self, Susanne effectively dismantled gender norms and demonstrated that the journey towards inclusive leadership is inherently tied to unleashing creativity and innovation.

Through her story, we are reminded that within every challenge lies an opportunity, and within every setback lies the growth potential. Susanne's journey beckons us to unleash the creativity within and ignite the fires of innovation, one courageous step at a time.

Invention Has Nothing to Do with Our Gender

Here, we shatter the notion that invention has any gender boundaries, for creativity knows no limits, confines, or labels. Let's dive deep into the depths of our minds, where assumptions lurk like mischievous shadows, whispering that certain genders possess an innate aptitude for innovation.

Creating the Future

You can create a futuristic fairground where ideas are thrilling rides. The roller coasters of innovation defy gravity, and the carousel of creativity spins with dazzling colours.

So, I ask you: In what year would you like to see the concept of the new leadership rules beyond gender as natural as breathing?

This means living in a world where cultures have embraced this paradigm shift, and gender biases are but tales of the past. Men, women, and non-binary individuals—every leader dances in the realm of creativity and innovation, unburdened by outdated stereotypes.

In this utopian vision, gender is no longer a prism through which we perceive capability. It's not just young men heralded as the torchbearers of AI and IT innovation, middle-aged white men in boardrooms, or women in caregiver roles. Instead, individuals of all ages, backgrounds, and genders fuel the engines of ingenuity. Our canvas of possibility is painted with strokes of inclusivity, and the symphony of ideas knows no gender-based notes.

The New Rules of Leadership at Home

Would you like to live in a world where parents take 100 percent equal roles in raising their children? A world where both parents get to lead by example, work on their careers, and raise their families equally? It's a world where it's normal to see both men and women taking responsibility for the third watch—the mental shift that entails remembering all the appointments, birthdays, school assignments, and doctors' appointments!

The New Rules of Leadership at Your Workplace

Would you like to see ambitious women and caring men more equally in leadership positions? Would you like to live in a world where it's just as ordinary to see women in IT as it is to see men in caregiving roles?

Would you like to live in a society where all the above is as expected, and the community has created the base for this?

If you said yes to any of these questions, I've got to ask you another fundamental question.

Would you like to see this in your lifetime? Do you see this as a utopian vision that might become a reality in your ancestor's lifetime, perhaps in the year 3000?

Your actions today will determine the future.

In the grand tapestry of shaping a world beyond gender boundaries, the power of envisioning cannot be underestimated.

You see, your vision matters!

Your innovative mind matters!

It's like having a compass that guides us through uncharted waters, steering us towards the shores of transformation. Our imaginations are the architects of innovation, weaving threads of possibility into the fabric of reality.

Just as the theory of the quantum field suggests, the creation process begins within the chambers of our minds before it manifests in the physical realm.

When we dare to dream and envision a world where gender is no longer a barrier to leadership, we tap into the boundless potential of the universe. The fusion of our thoughts, intentions, and actions catalyses the change we yearn to see. So, let's paint a vivid picture of a world brimming with equality and inclusivity, for our imagination is the brush that colours our reality.

Stay Open to the Possibilities

Diversity, in all dimensions, is a cornerstone of creativity and innovation within the leadership framework beyond gender.

The fusion of perspectives, backgrounds, and experiences from many sources cultivates a fertile ground for developing novel ideas and transformative solutions.

When we broaden the scope of diversity beyond just gender, embracing differences in race, ethnicity, socioeconomic background, and more, we embark on a journey that fuels the creative process.

I'm not saying it's easy to do this. I'm encouraging you to look at your current mindset and struggles in creating this space.

The amalgamation of varied viewpoints challenges conventional thinking and encourages a broader exploration of possibilities. It's akin to a symphony where each unique note contributes to the harmonious composition of innovation.

By fostering an environment where diverse voices are heard and valued, we unlock the door to a treasure trove of insights that pave the way for more comprehensive, thoughtful, and ingenious solutions. In this realm of leadership, creativity thrives in the rich tapestry of diversity, leading to a transformative impact that transcends traditional boundaries and propels us into a realm of boundless potential.

You Are the Trailblazer of Transformation

As leaders journeying beyond the confines of gender, we are not merely visionaries; we are the torchbearers of transformation. Leading by example is our canvas, where the strokes of our actions paint a vivid picture of a future we envision.

It's not just about saying, "Let's be creative." It's about creating an environment where innovation flourishes organically. The fusion of mindset and action brews the elixir of transformation.

To cultivate innovation, we must first discard the notions that creativity has an age, a gender, or a predefined path. Think of invention as a rebellious child, unafraid to question norms and explore the uncharted. Embrace diversity in all its forms, for it's the diversity of thought that fuels the furnace of creativity.

It's about embodying the change we seek and inspiring others to follow.

In this world we are crafting, strengths are illuminated without the shadows of gender assumptions. We become the living embodiment of the truth that potential knows no gender and that each individual's capabilities flourish when nurtured without preconceived notions. By embracing this ethos, we foster a culture that acknowledges talents for what they are— unique expressions of human potential, untethered by the outdated limitations of gender stereotypes.

The good news is that you will fail!

But let's not stop there. Let's shift our perspective on failure. Instead of fearing it, let's see it as a stepping-stone to innovate a world where people are valued for their strengths, not their genders.

Failure is the precursor to growth, the herald of break-throughs. Imagine a world where failure is celebrated, where leaders wear their failed attempts like badges of honour, a testament to their courage to push boundaries.

In this enchanting realm of imagination, innovation sprawls beyond the confines of exclusivity; it's a grand feast of ideas where leaders beyond gender roles ensure every individual has a seat reserved at the table.

It's a world where creativity flourishes from the start, schools become incubators of innovation, and these trailblazing leaders wholeheartedly urge children to explore, experiment, and dream beyond the stars.

Let's conclude this journey with five sparkling takeaways:

1. **Unleash the Imagination:** Break free from assumptions and let creativity soar without gender boundaries.

2. **Embrace Diversity:** Mix and mingle minds from all walks of life for the diverse symphony that orchestrates innovation.

3. **Reimagine Failure:** Turn failure into a stepping-stone, an essential ingredient in the innovation recipe.

4. **Democratise Creativity:** Invite everyone to the creative banquet. Innovation needs no VIP passes.

5. **Nurture Young Minds:** Cultivate a culture of innovation from childhood, turning schools into gardens of creative exploration.

And now, for the pièce de résistance, three questions beckon you to shape the world you envision:

1. How can you amplify the voices of creative leaders who defy gender stereotypes in your industry?

2. What's one assumption about creativity and gender you can challenge in your leadership journey?

3. Envision a world where gender biases are extinct. What role can you play today to bring that vision closer to reality?

So, fellow visionaries, it's time to unleash your imagination and ride the roller coaster of innovation. We shape the world through creativity, unlocking doors to endless possibilities.

Unleash your imagination!

And so, as we conclude this chapter, let the words of Susanne Frandsen echo in our hearts: Unleash your imagination, for it is through creativity that we shape the world and open doors to endless possibilities.

Just as Susanne's journey reminds us, the canvas of leadership beyond gender is painted not only with determination and resilience but also with the vibrant colours of innovation.

As we navigate the waters of self-discovery and transformation, let us carry the torch of creativity, igniting the flames of change and embracing infinite horizons. The path of leadership is about steering our ships through challenges and navigating with the compass of our unique ideas and perspectives.

So, my fellow explorers of leadership's uncharted realms, let your imagination be your guiding star, lighting the way towards a future illuminated by the boundless potential of your creativity.

Remember, the future is a canvas waiting for your brushstrokes of change.

CHAPTER 14

Redefining Success:
Beyond Traditional Metrics

In a world where titles and accolades often measure success,
what if we redefine it as a journey of personal fulfilment,
positive impact, and holistic achievement?
With the new leadership rules,
we dance to the rhythm of our values
and celebrate the beauty of diverse perspectives.

What if you could redefine success for yourself?

A new chapter with a topic that has been a transformational journey for me personally to ponder.

I embrace the wisdom shared by Gido Schimanski: ***"Life is happening for us, not to us."***

This perspective empowers us to redefine success beyond traditional metrics as leaders beyond genders. It gives us space to break free from societal expectations and measure success by personal fulfilment, well-being, and positive impact.

Liberated from a one-size-fits-all concept, we lead authentically, celebrating diverse paths.

With this mindset and worldview, we can pave the way for an inclusive and compassionate approach to success, empowering ourselves and those we lead to thrive.

Life is happening for us and is redefined beyond norms, guiding us on a transformative journey as leaders beyond genders.

Today, we're breaking free from the shackles of traditional metrics and stepping into a realm of success uniquely ours. Success isn't a cookie-cutter concept, and it certainly isn't limited to the confines of societal expectations.

We are redefining success on our terms and embracing a holistic approach encompassing personal fulfilment, well-being, and positive impact.

Now, let's take a moment to examine the traditional metrics of success that have been drilled into us since we were kids. A hefty pay check, a prestigious title, and a corner office— that's the dream, right?

Do these external markers truly define your success? Or is there something more profound that aligns with your core values and purpose?

Embracing the new leadership rules, we must recognise that our value systems need a revamp. If we want, we can let go of the notion that success is solely about material achievements. While those things are lovely, they're just one piece of the puzzle. We, however, can easily fall into the trap of believing that success is defined by our money in the bank or even how much we owe the bank, strangely enough— ingrained **gender roles based on habits and rituals.**

Our social conditioning and ingrained gender roles often impose limiting beliefs, making us believe we must fulfil certain functions based on our genders. This conditioning can hinder our ability to measure success holistically.

For example, traditionally, men have been expected to be the primary breadwinners, valuing financial success above all else, regardless of how good or bad they are at it!

On the other hand, women have often been confined to domestic roles, with their success measured by how well they manage their households and caregiving responsibilities, regardless of their capacity to be in that role.

This system has not exactly been helping us be the best version of ourselves. It's been restricting us!

These narrow definitions of success can suffocate, leaving little room for personal growth and fulfilment beyond these prescribed roles. It's holding us stuck in very tiny boxes, with minimal space to get fresh air for us to breathe and rejuvenate.

However, when we expand our boxes or even break free from the restrictions of gender norms and embrace the wisdom that life is happening for us, not to us, we open ourselves up to a world of possibilities.

As leaders beyond genders, we are redefining success on our terms, taking into account our unique strengths, passions, and values.

For instance, a man who was once confined by societal expectations of being stoic and emotionally reserved may find true success in expressing vulnerability and embracing emotional intelligence!

Similarly, a woman limited by expectations to be submissive and passive may discover her success in becoming a powerful advocate and leader in her field.

By shedding the shackles of traditional gender roles, we empower ourselves to measure success more meaningfully and fully. Success becomes about personal growth, well-being, and positive impact rather than conforming to rigid norms.

As leaders, we should embrace a more inclusive and compassionate approach, valuing the diverse paths that individuals choose to pursue.

To do so effectively, we must train ourselves to build our self-awareness muscles and react more mindfully to things and circumstances.

In this new paradigm, success is no longer confined by gender stereotypes but reflects our authentic selves.

As we lead with this perspective, we create an environment where others feel empowered to do the same. By redefining success beyond traditional metrics, we foster an inclusive and supportive culture that celebrates individuality and diverse expressions of leadership.

In conclusion, breaking free from societal conditioning and rigid gender roles is a transformative step towards redefining success as leaders beyond genders. Embracing the wisdom that life is happening for us, not to us, allows us to measure success in a way that aligns with our unique values and aspirations.

By dismantling traditional gender norms, we pave the way for more holistic and fulfilling paths to success for ourselves and those we lead.

Can you imagine the impact you, alone, can make when you embrace this new perspective? Becoming a catalyst for positive change and inspiring others to embark on their journeys of growth and self-discovery?

True success lies in finding harmony between our personal and professional lives, nurturing our well-being, and positively impacting the world.

Redefining Success in Self-Leadership and Leading Others

When redefining success beyond genders, there is a distinct difference between self-leadership and leading others.

Self-Leadership

Self-leadership involves breaking free from societal conditioning and redefining success on our own terms. It is about understanding our unique values, passions, and aspirations and aligning our actions with those internal compasses. In this process, we liberate ourselves from the limitations of traditional gender roles, allowing us to measure success in a more holistic and fulfilling way.

Leading Your Team or Organisation

On the other hand, leading others in the context of redefining success requires empathy, compassion, and a deep understanding of individuality. As leaders beyond genders, we must first work hard on our listening skills. You need to be able to listen even to unsaid things. Deep, active listening skills will help you to understand others.

Understanding your own value system is the next step. Once you know what you stand for and can create a safe space for others to flourish in, you can create an inclusive and supportive environment where team members can pursue their own paths to success. It involves recognising and celebrating diverse expressions of leadership and empowering others to break free from societal norms and embrace their authentic selves.

In essence, self-leadership is the foundation for leading others in a way that transcends gender expectations. By redefining success personally, we can extend that same freedom and encouragement to those we lead, creating a culture of empowerment and growth.

A powerful synergy between individual transformation and collective support leads us to a more inclusive and thriving leadership paradigm!

Five Takeaways

So, let's dive into five points that illustrate the transformative power of redefining success:

1. **Rediscovering Our Purpose:** When we redefine success, we prioritise our purpose over external validations. Regularly ask yourself, "What truly brings me joy and fulfilment as a leader?" Whether it's making a difference in our community, inspiring others through mentorship, or fostering a collaborative work environment, our purpose becomes the guiding star that leads us to meaningful achievements.

2. **Embracing Well-Being:** Success isn't just about burning the candle at both ends and sacrificing our health for professional gains. That perspective was once a virtue; don't fall into that old paradigm created by dead people! Instead, we value our well-being and understand that self-care is a non-negotiable aspect of effective leadership. Look deeply at how you can prioritise rest, exercise, and mindfulness, knowing that a healthy and balanced leader is a more impactful leader.

3. **Making an Impact:** Beyond traditional metrics, success is about leaving a positive mark on the world. As leaders beyond genders, we aim to create inclusive environments that empower others to thrive. That environment can be both in your home and your workplace. We measure our success by our transformative impact on our families, friends, teams, organisations, and communities.

4. **Resilience and Adaptability:** In our pursuit of success, we embrace the inevitability of challenges

and setbacks. Remember, *life is always happening for you, not to you.* We develop resilience and adaptability, knowing that it's not about avoiding obstacles but how we navigate through them that defines our success.

5. **Leading by Example:** Redefining success starts with us. As leaders, we must embody the values and principles we wish to see in our families, friends, teams, and organisations. When we prioritise well-being, purpose, and impact, we inspire those around us.

Can you see now how crucial it is to start with ourselves when redefining success?

Success is an inside job, and it begins with a shift in our mindset and values. We can only authentically lead others towards a new definition of success by embracing it ourselves.

You are redefining your success!

As we embark on this journey of redefining success, remember that it's not about achieving a particular milestone or reaching a certain level of recognition. It's not confined to a single, standardised tune in the grand symphony of success. Success is as diverse as the vibrant hues of a rainbow, each shade representing a unique journey.

Align yourself with the rhythm of your own heart, and in every small victory, embrace the melody of your efforts. These are not just small wins; they are the breadcrumbs leading you to the masterpiece that is your success story.

Celebrate every note, every step, and every moment of growth, for it's in the tapestry of these experiences that your authentic success is woven. It's about the everyday moments of growth, connection, and joy that make up the tapestry of our leadership.

The challenge redefining your success beyond the traditional metrics.

Navigating the path to redefine success beyond traditional metrics is challenging. Breaking away from ingrained gender roles and societal expectations can be daunting, as individuals often face resistance from both within and outside.

Overcoming the fear of judgement, self-doubt, and the pressure to conform can be a significant hurdle. Fulfilling a solid sense of self-awareness becomes crucial to triumph over these obstacles.

For me personally, writing this book has been a frightening experience. I've had to turn my fear into encouragement as I've found my monkey mind. You know, that inner voice that keeps telling you stuff that's not helpful for you to listen to when facing a challenge. I've had sleepless nights, pondering over thoughts, wondering what people will really think of me when they read the book, etc.

What has helped me enormously along the way are two things:

a) When in doubt, I go within and remind myself why I'm writing this book—and the image of my granddaughter's face pops up in my mind.

b) I also calm my nervous system by reminding myself that most likely she is going to be the only person who will read it anyway. Yes, this is how I use humour for myself.

Self-reflection allows us to recognise our authentic values, passions, and aspirations and empowers us to build resilience in the face of adversity.

Moreover, embracing this new definition of success can spark a ripple effect beyond personal growth. By challenging gender norms, we contribute to reshaping organisational culture and societal norms, fostering environments where diverse expressions of leadership are celebrated.

This, in turn, creates a more inclusive and compassionate world where success is measured by individual achievements and our positive impact on those around us and the broader community.

Ready to step into the arena with courage and an open heart and redefine your success?

CHAPTER 15

Cultivating a Culture of Belonging:
Being Seen, Valued, and Respected

True leadership is not confined by gender,
but flourishes in the inclusive garden of authenticity,
where each individual's uniqueness is celebrated,
and the symphony of diverse voices
creates a harmony of belonging.

Greetings, fellow travellers on the path of transformation!

Today, our compass points us towards the radiant shores of inclusive environments and the lush landscapes of belonging.

But let's pause for a moment before we dive into the heart of this chapter and ask a question that reverberates with significance: Is the banner of diversity, equity, and inclusion (DEI) simply a catchy slogan?

This buzzword sounds good but needs more actual depth. Or are we genuinely prepared to delve into the depths of this concept, unravel the complexities behind our struggles, and confront why we've been depriving ourselves of the full spectrum of skills, talents, experiences, and passions that humanity possesses?

As we enter this chapter, let's peel away the layers and examine our surroundings.

Questions We Need to Ask Ourselves Regularly

Are we willing to do more than scratch the surface of diversity and inclusion? Can we muster the courage to plunge into the core of this matter, to challenge our assumptions and to dismantle the walls that have confined us to limited viewpoints and actions?

Reflect on the substantial investments in DEI initiatives across industries.

Are these investments merely a formality, a checklist to mark off? Or do businesses and organisations sincerely yearn for a transformation?

Are they ready to embrace the richness of a diverse workforce, foster leadership beyond the boundaries of gender, and break free from the confines of traditional roles and expectations?

Let's illuminate this path with the lantern of self-examination. Are we indeed prepared for the journey that extends beyond superficial diversity and delves into the essence of what it means to create inclusive environments?

Can we commit to shattering the gender-based assumptions that have held us captive and recognise that authentic leadership transcends these limiting categories?

Will we allocate resources not just for show but for substantial training and development that nurtures leaders who champion authenticity, inclusion, and growth?

All oversized and relevant questions that need clarity!

As we embark on this chapter, let's keep this inquiry at the forefront of our minds. Are we content with dipping our toes into the waters of diversity and inclusion, or are we ready to plunge into the depths, exploring the profound changes this transformation can bring?

The journey is rife with both challenges and rewards—an inclusive world where each individual's potential is celebrated, where leadership defies gender stereotypes, and where our collective potential flourishes.

Is DEI Just Another Box?

Now, let's weave an additional thread into this tapestry.

How much does it cost our societies to use only a fraction of the human potential?

What if we consider the cost of upholding gender stereotype roles and boxes? What if we reflect on this perspective's toll on businesses, organisations, communities, and entire countries?

The Organisation for Economic Co-operation and Development [OECD] estimation speaks volumes about the untapped potential within our grasp. The prospect of adding $28 trillion to the global GDP by 2025 through women's equal economic participation underscores the urgency of embracing inclusive environments. This potential is particularly potent in developing countries, where the impact can be transformational.

To expedite the journey towards this stage of inclusive leadership, we must focus on the future leaders who will pave the way.

Through education, awareness, and empowerment programs—not just for women but for all genders—we can equip the next generation with the tools to shatter gender norms, challenge biases, and champion a culture of belonging.

By nurturing minds of all ages with equality, respect, and authentic leadership, we can accelerate progress and usher in an era where leadership transcends gender, and the symphony of diverse voices leads us towards a harmonious and prosperous future.

This isn't just a theoretical pondering; it's a matter of grave significance.

I'm a bit like a broken record here. Bear with me, please.

When we confine individuals to predefined roles based on their gender, we rob ourselves of the full scope of their capabilities. We perpetuate unequal skills, talents, and experience distribution, hampering our collective growth.

This isn't merely a philosophical dilemma; it has financial implications.

So, as we delve into this chapter, let's embrace these questions and weave their essence into our exploration.

Let's recognise the gravity of our choices and acknowledge that fostering inclusive environments isn't just a feel-good pursuit; it's necessary for the growth and success of individuals, organisations, and societies.

As we traverse this path, let's do so with a heightened awareness of the profound changes we can affect by championing leadership beyond gender, cultivating cultures of inclusivity, and embracing the talents and potential that know no gender bounds.

Bringing in Diversity by Embracing People's Energies, Not Their Genders!

In pursuing a genuinely inclusive team environment, as I discussed in chapter 4, Nick Haines's ancient Chinese wisdom on the five energies provides a captivating perspective that can help us on the journey towards diversity and inclusive teams.

These energies, namely wood, fire, earth, metal, and water, symbolise the diverse facets of human nature and its interactions. You can think of the wood energy as embodying innovation and growth, while the earth energy exudes stability and support, for example.

By understanding and embracing the concept of these elemental energies, leaders can nurture fundamental diversity within their teams. Just as each element contributes to the harmonious balance of nature, each energy type contributes to the dynamic balance of a cohesive team.

Recognising and valuing these elemental strengths present within the team is pivotal to cultivating a culture of belonging. This means acknowledging diverse energies—not genders— and seeing how they contribute to the collaborative tapestry.

Are We Being Seen, Valued, and Respected?

Here are some actionable steps or strategies for individuals and organisations to cultivate a culture of belonging.

For individuals, start by actively seeking diverse perspectives and engaging in open conversations that encourage sharing and understanding.

Research has shown that teams with diverse viewpoints are more innovative and effective.

Additionally, as I've already talked about, practice inclusive language and behaviours that make everyone feel valued and respected, such as addressing individuals by their preferred pronouns and acknowledging their contributions.

Organisations can implement mentorship and sponsorship programs that support underrepresented groups, fostering a sense of belonging and upward mobility.

For instance, through mentorship initiatives, Hewlett-Packard set the goal to increase the number of women in leadership by 50 percent. Also, regular diversity and inclusion training can help teams recognise and address biases, creating a more inclusive atmosphere. Encouraging flexible work arrange- ments and parental leave policies can also contribute to inclusivity, allowing individuals to balance their personal and professional lives.

By taking these tangible steps, individuals and organisations can cultivate a culture of belonging that celebrates diversity and empowers everyone to lead beyond gender expectations.

When leaders foster an environment where each energy is respected and integrated, they create a space where every team member feels welcomed and truly valued. This empowerment enables everyone to contribute their distinctive viewpoints, unleashing a synergy of creativity and innovation that propels the team towards success.

Five Core Takeaways:

1. **Authentic Leadership Drives Inclusivity:** From the top down, leaders must embrace authenticity, creating a haven for their team members to express themselves genuinely.

2. **Embrace Diversity as a Strength:** Celebrate individual uniqueness and diverse perspectives, allowing each contribution to enrich the whole.

3. **Mindful Communication for Active Listening:** Cultivate conscious communication, opening the doors to authentic connections where every voice matters.

4. **Breaking Free from Gender Norms:** Challenge traditional gender norms and embrace an inclusive approach that empowers individuals to bring their authentic selves to the table.

5. **Allyship and Advocacy in Action:** Active allyship fosters inclusivity. Uplift marginalised voices, amplify their strengths, and stand against discrimination and bias.

As we conclude this transformative chapter on fostering inclusive environments and cultivating a culture of belonging, let's remind ourselves that authentic leadership beyond gender isn't just about breaking barriers but building bridges. It's about creating spaces where every individual can thrive, where diversity is tolerated and celebrated, and where collaboration flourishes.

By championing a culture of belonging, we pave the way for a future where gender is no longer a barrier to leadership excellence. It's a journey that calls us to challenge our biases, honour our differences, and uplift one another.

So, let us continue to be the architects of change, the champions of unity, and the leaders illuminating the path for others to follow.

Together, we shape a world where everyone's voice matters, every unique perspective is valued, and the true power of leadership shines through the tapestry of human diversity.

Chapter 16

The Gift of Mentorship: Empowering the Next Generation

In this chapter, we'll unlock the transformative power of mentorship as mentors and mentees. We'll explore the impact of mentorship on personal growth, skill development, and the cultivation of diverse leadership styles. Prepare to pay it forward and become a guiding light for those who come after us.

Ah, mentorship—the precious gift we pass on to the next generation of leaders. In this chapter, get ready to unlock the transformative power of mentorship, both as mentors and mentees. Together, we'll dive deep into the impact of mentorship on personal growth, skill development, and the cultivation of diverse leadership styles.

One of my most giant lottery wins in life is having mentors!

My journey with Dr. David Paul and Nick Haines—my No More Boxes Transformational Movement partners—has been illuminating.

Each conversation with them has been a profound journey of discovery as I gain deeper insights into human behaviours and untapped potentials through their lenses of mindfulness, neuroscience, and energy fields.

For me, it's as if every interaction is a winning ticket to the grandest lottery prize.

Yet, what adds an even greater layer of fulfilment is knowing that our exchange is reciprocal. As I share my experiences and perspectives with them, I witness how those contributions become actionable elements in their lives. This cycle of empowerment, inspiration, and trust creates an endless growth loop, fuelling our collective commitment to shaping a better future.

The intertwining of our insights forms a symphony of transformation, and I am deeply grateful for the privilege of experiencing this journey alongside such remarkable minds.

The Fulfilment of Being a Mentor

One of my favourite roles is being a mentor for someone. I've been so fortunate to do that as a leadership coach and mentor for entrepreneurs, business leaders, and people in the political arena. Being their shadow, that person standing by their side, is a priceless experience.

If you have lived a life as a professional in just about anything—it could be a professional mum or dad, for that matter—but if you are a professional, you've got something to give back to those who have not had the experience you have. So, let's prepare to pay it forward and become guiding lights for those who come after us.

Here are five strategies to foster a leader who leads beyond gender:

Strategy 1: Embrace Unconventional Pairings

When leading beyond gender, let's challenge the traditional mentorship roles society has placed upon us. Instead of sticking to gender norms, let's embrace unconventional pairings that defy expectations.

Women mentor men, and men mentor women. It's time to break free from the confines of outdated gender roles. By fostering cross-gender mentorship, we empower the mentees to see beyond stereotypes and open doors for diverse leadership styles to emerge.

In the past, mentorship has often followed a predictable pattern—male mentors guiding males and female mentors supporting female mentees.

In some cultures, this ritual can feel like an unwritten rule. As you've most likely noticed in this book, we must constantly revisit our habits, routines, and behaviours and check in regularly to see if they are still the best thing for everyone! Also, as our brain wants to do the easy thing in life—meaning the same thing it has always done—one has to be aware of our self-talk. We will always make excuses not to change whatever feels "normal" to us.

I'm not saying there is anything wrong with all of the old approaches. However, I want to highlight the richness it can give both mentor and mentee to work together, regardless of gender.

We all bring different approaches to the world. By supporting another person, sharing your experience, and simultaneously allowing them to figure out how they want to proceed, we are giving them insights into our world.

As a woman mentor, you will be able to give a male mentee insights from your experience as a woman leader, and the same goes for you as a male mentor, mentoring both men and women.

Imagine the impact of stepping out of these predefined roles and mixing things up. By embracing unconventional pairings, we create opportunities for diverse perspectives and fresh insights to flourish. The richness of mentorship lies in the diversity of experiences, not in conforming to societal expectations.

Strategy 2: Bring in Richness and Mutual Understanding

When we embrace unconventional pairings in mentorship, we pave the way for a more inclusive and dynamic leadership culture. We can start to understand each other more deeply, and not just from what we assume a person brings to the table based on their gender.

No longer limited by gender norms, mentors and mentees can connect on a deeper level, free from preconceived notions. As a mentor, your wisdom and guidance become accessible to mentees of all genders. As a mentee, you can seek inspiration from leaders who resonate with your vision, regardless of gender.

Strategy 3: Celebrate Vulnerability and Authenticity

"Vulnerability is not winning or losing; it dares to show up and be seen when we have no control over the outcome." —Brené Brown.

As mentors, let's create safe spaces where vulnerability and authenticity are celebrated. Gone are the days of pretending to have all the answers.

Why is it okay to be a leader and sometimes be afraid? This is one of my favourite Conscious Questions by my business partner and friend, Nick Haines.

Let's show our mentees that it's okay not to be perfect and that growth comes from embracing our vulnerabilities. Sharing our struggles and triumphs paves the way for honest and meaningful connections.

Remember, it's not about projecting an image of invincibility but about being genuine and relatable leaders.

Strategy 4: Empower the Next Generation to Lead with Your Heart and Mind . . . and Gut!

Beyond genders, let's encourage the next generation of leaders to lead with heart, mind, and soul. You might have heard the term to speak from your heart or lead from your heart, and in some cases, it seems as if we are being told to forget our mind in decision-making. I like to see it as an encouragement to learn to trust your intuition more than you might have been raised to do, but that doesn't mean you should not use your mind at all. Our mind is there for a reason, just as our heart . . . and even our guts are!

Sound strange? Trust me, you have all of it: a heart, mind, and gut. Why not connect and use all three?

Stragety 5: Install a sense of purpose and passion

Mentorship is not just about teaching technical skills; it's about instilling a sense of purpose and passion. Let's empower our mentees to be compassionate, empathetic, and inclusive leaders who lead with a deep understanding of the human experience. When they lead with heart, mind, gut, and I'm even going to add in leading from their soul's purpose, they can create meaningful and sustainable change, leaving a lasting impact on the world.

As we embark on this mentorship journey, we must recognise that being a mentor becomes a part of our personal brand.

The ripple effect is profound when we are known for mentoring the future generation to become even better leaders. Our legacy extends beyond our achievements, reaching the farthest corners of the leadership landscape.

Mentorship that follows the new leadership rules beyond gender is a powerful force that defies stereotypes and expectations. By transcending traditional mentorship roles, we pave the way for a more inclusive and dynamic leadership culture. We celebrate diversity and embrace each individual's unique contributions, regardless of gender.

In this realm of mentorship, the focus is not on what makes us different but what unites us as leaders—our interconnectedness and shared commitment to growth, empowerment, and positively impacting the world.

The captivating world of leadership beyond gender illuminates the radiant gift of mentorship, a torch we pass fervently to ignite the paths of emerging leaders.

As pioneers of progress, we find wisdom in the words of Leslie Grossman, eloquently shared in *The Change Makers Podcast,* episode #5. Leslie beckons us to embrace the concept that building our entourage is akin to curating an invaluable council of mentors. Her insights paint a vibrant tapestry of leadership, where no ascent is solitary, and none of us stands alone.

The episode resonates with the harmonious truth that leaders, regardless of gender, flourish within a trusted network. Here, Leslie artfully weaves the essence of leadership, emphasising that collaboration, companionship, and mutual growth are the heartbeat of success. She guides us through the art of networking, revealing strategies to navigate its terrain with grace and authenticity.

Leslie's wisdom resonates profoundly from the power of a friendly companion at events to engaging in conversations with a genuine curiosity for others' stories. Leslie Grossman's insights ripple as a testament: mentorship, both given and received, fortifies the foundation upon which leadership excellence is built, a symphony that empowers and endures.

To sum up the three core takeaways from this chapter:

1. Embrace unconventional pairings to break free from outdated gender norms and foster diverse leadership styles.

2. Create safe spaces for vulnerability and authenticity, leading by example to inspire genuine connections.

3. Empower the next generation to lead with heart and soul, instilling a sense of purpose and compassion in their leadership.

Three questions to ask yourself as you evolve into becoming a leader beyond genders:

1. How can I challenge traditional mentorship roles and embrace unconventional pairings to foster a more inclusive leadership culture?

2. What steps can I take as a mentor to create a safe space for vulnerability and authenticity, allowing my mentees to thrive and grow?

3. What feeling do I want to leave behind in other people's minds and hearts at the end of this day?

Let's wrap up chapter 16!

In this poignant culmination of chapter 16, we stand on the precipice of a transformational truth: mentorship is the timeless gift we lovingly bequeath to the next generation of leaders. Within these pages, we've unravelled the delicate artistry of mentorship, a gift bestowed with purpose and intention.

As we pass this torch, we embrace the wisdom shared by trailblazers like Leslie Grossman, a beacon of insight in *The Change Makers Podcast,* episode #5. Leslie's knowledge resonates with a clarion call to build our entourage, crafting an invaluable council of mentors from diverse realms.

Here, we grasp that leadership's tapestry knows no bounds of gender; collaboration, companionship, and mutual growth are the heartbeats of our journey. Navigating the networking terrain, we adopt strategies honouring authenticity and empowering our interactions.

Be aware you are not building a network of people who look like you!

As much as I love and adore the many women I've met throughout my life at women's conferences who've served as examples and included me in their women's networks, I've also faced the sad consequences of that one narrow network. I was only connected with women in the business world, not men.

Noticing I had fallen into the trap of just staying in my tight little box of women's network wasn't giving me access to the wealth men could give me on my journey in the business world, I realised that my network needed to be more expansive in the business world outside of just the women's part.

Is a women's network opening up for men to join in?

We've got to be able to hold space for two things simultaneously. Many older men's clubs, such as the Lions, the Rotary, or Oddfellows, started as men's only clubs, in later years they have either created a special women's clubs, or even opened them up for any gender. We still have not seen international women's clubs do the same for men.

Following the new rules of leadership is also about bringing in men where they have not been invited just as much as it is about bringing women into roles that society has not seen them capable of flourishing in.

When women's networks can invite men who share their values, visions, and passions for a different kind of world, things will open up for men to build their diverse network as well.

Mentorship's ripple of influence extends beyond gender confines; it strengthens leadership foundations, empowering voices to reverberate across time and space.

We sculpt a legacy that transcends expectations by embracing unconventional pairings, fostering safe spaces for vulnerability, and imparting the essence of leading with heart and soul.

This chapter has beckoned you to engage with these truths and leave the echoes of mentorship's transformative resonance behind.

CHAPTER 17

Leading with Integrity: Ethical Decision-Making

Ethics and integrity aren't mere concepts; they're the essence of remarkable leadership. This chapter delves into the heart of ethical decision-making, guided by our unwavering commitment to our core values.

Leading with Integrity

Ethical decision-making is the soul of the new rules of leadership beyond gender. It involves recognising the influence of our core values, beliefs, and principles in shaping our choices. Leading with integrity starts within—a journey of understanding our true north and being candid with ourselves.

But it doesn't end there. Leaders steering teams or organisations must constantly remind themselves to broaden their horizons. We must always question our assumptions as our assumptions will always be marked by our background, education, culture, status, and so forth. In other words, our unconscious programming. Being constantly aware that 95 percent of your behaviours are run by your unconscious programs . . . that's a lot!

It's about asking open-ended questions to actively seek diverse viewpoints, empathising with the potential impact of our choices, and cultivating an atmosphere of open dialogue.

My Ethical Journey: Staying True to Freedom and Value

Staying true to ethical principles has been empowering and challenging. My core values of freedom and being of value have guided me through the maze of decision-making. Writing this book is a testament to my commitment to these values. Yet, staying the course has its challenges. I've faced the fear of rejection, being judged, and ridiculed even by close friends and family as I held steadfast to my mission. Embracing ethical leadership can mean confronting our fears and insecurities, and my journey reflects that struggle and triumph.

Navigating Everyday Ethical Decisions and Change in Approach

Ethical decision-making isn't confined to our work life or boardroom; it's woven into the fabric of our daily lives. My guest on *The Change Makers* podcast episode 154, Mahmud Samandari, from Soul.com, shared his experience of transforming a company gathering by inviting people to share their thoughts and ideas instead of giving a traditional talk. This shift led to new and exciting ideas that individuals could implement independently. Our school systems and society have taught us that you must have the answers for everything. Listening to understand one another, including having conversations around what ethics means to us, can lead to an entirely new culture inside your business, organisation, and even your home if that's the conversation at your kitchen table.

Championing Diversity and Inclusivity

Leadership beyond gender embraces diversity at its core. Ethical leadership encourages us to welcome varied perspectives and experiences, ensuring our decisions are unbiased and just. I resonated deeply with Mahmud Samandari's words when he shared his belief that human beings have no black-or-white relationships. Seeing each other as a combination of different skills, insights, knowledge, and backgrounds with a proactive approach is much more likely to give us harmony and well-being than believing our old perceptions.

Continuous Growth and Transparency

Ethical leadership is an ongoing journey of growth. I'm sorry, my friend, but the day you graduate from this continuing education journey, that's the day you die!

We must stay informed about industry best practices, actively engage in workshops and seminars, and seek guidance from our personal coaches, mentors, and role models. Moreover, ethical leaders invest in emotional intelligence, empathy, and active listening. These qualities enable us to connect with others more profoundly, make decisions that prioritise our team's well-being, and foster trust.

Leading by Example: The Heart of Ethical Leadership

Leading by example is at the core of ethical leadership. When we consistently demonstrate integrity through our actions, we send a resounding message to our teams, inspiring them to emulate these values. Trust in bringing about change is essential. Emphasise listening and thinking about the significant purpose of your team or community. Give yourself and your team time and space to reflect and have meaningful conversations to generate trust.

Creating an Ethical Culture

Creating an ethical culture thrives on collaboration, teamwork, and diverse perspectives. As leaders, we encourage open dialogue, celebrate constructive dissent, and weigh various viewpoints to make informed decisions. External pressures, such as financial constraints, can test our ethical resolve. In these moments, prioritising ethics over short-term gains is crucial, reminding us that our principles should guide our choices. Finding the courage to talk about the issue non-judgementally can help immensely.

A Journey Beyond Societal Norms

In closing, ethical decision-making exemplifies leadership beyond gender. It transcends societal norms and expectations. My podcast guest, Mahmud Samandari, asserts that society needs to utilise everyone's capacities and talents fully. The call for creating conditions and spaces where everyone's ability can be developed and used must be answered.

How do you do all these things? You are just a human being, right?

To help you out, I'll share my daily checklist, which I like to read before I go to bed, reflecting on my day. It helps me stay true to myself and gives me guidelines for what I need to focus on next.

My Five-Step Daily Ethical Culture Implementation Checklist

- **Values Alignment:**

  I align my actions with my core values daily, ensuring I live and lead by ethical principles.

- **Open Dialogue:**

  I foster open and honest dialogue within my family and team, valuing diverse perspectives and encouraging constructive discussions.

- **Leading by Example:**

  I consistently strive to set an example of ethical behaviour, demonstrating it in all aspects of my life and leadership.

- **Embrace Diversity:**

  I actively embrace diversity in my team and my life, recognising the value it brings to decision-making and innovation.

- **Reflect and Impact:**

  I regularly reflect on the impact of my ethical choices, considering how they contribute to a positive work environment and a fairer, more inclusive world.

There are plenty of days that I see I didn't manage to do all of this, and that's fine.

What matters is awareness, noting what I accomplished, self-leadership, and not beating up the earlier version of myself. When I notice in my daily reflections that I didn't do something as I would have wanted to do, I can consciously choose how I will behave differently next time. It's not failure; it's a possibility of expansion and growth.

In closing, as we stand at the intersection of ethics and leadership, remember that the unwavering torch of ethical integrity illuminates the journey to leadership. In ethical leadership, we don't merely navigate the waters; we set sail with a moral compass as our guide. As we close this chapter, remember that our choices are the keystones of our legacy, shaping a future defined by integrity and justice. By championing ethical decision-making, we forge a brighter tomorrow for ourselves and the people we influence.

CHAPTER 18

The Joy of Lifelong Learning: Embracing Growth, Adaptation, and AI

"Leadership beyond gender is an orchestra of authenticity, where the symphony of joy conducts the harmonious flow of individual brilliance." —Wendy Watkins.

Welcome to chapter 18! Congratulations on making it this far. In this chapter, we'll delve deep into the heart of leadership's ever-evolving dance, exploring how you can grow as a leader while embracing curiosity, active listening, and the power of AI. We'll also uncover the top skills projected for the future by the World Economic Forum. So, let's get started!

We have quite a lot to cover. To simplify things, I've divided this chapter into eight sections.

Section 1: The Path to Authentic Leadership

Leadership beyond gender is a symphony of authenticity, where the joy of embracing individual brilliance conducts harmonious progress. This section will explore the journey towards authentic leadership and the importance of self-awareness, self-leadership, self-love, and humour.

The 4-Step Out-Of-The-Box Formula from the No More Boxes Transformational Movement

Step 1: Self-awareness: Understanding your strengths, triggers, and passions is the first step towards authentic leadership. It helps you bring a fresh approach to leadership.

Step 2: Self-Leadership: Take control of your thoughts and actions, breaking free from societal norms, one step at a time.

Step 3: Self-Love: Embrace self-criticism with kindness and self-love. Your past self-brought you here; that's a gift.

Step 4: Humour for Self: Embrace mistakes with laughter, keeping an open and accepting energy.

Section 2: The Power of Curiosity

Let's clear up a common misconception—the idea that curiosity is harmful. Nonsense! Curiosity is the key that opens doors to meaningful connections and enriching conversations. We should break free from the belief that curiosity is bad and seen as being nosy.

In this section, we'll explore the importance of curiosity in leadership and how asking open-ended questions can help you understand your team better.

Curiosity breaks down barriers, builds bridges, and drives us to understand each other better. It's not nosy; it's a key to deeper connections.

Ask open questions about passions, values, and aspirations such as what are you passionate about or what do you value at work or in life? It all helps you know your team members better. It reveals their abilities, skills, experiences, passions, and values.

Section 3: Futureproofing Your Leadership Skills

The world is changing rapidly, as are the skills required in the workplace. In this section, we'll explore the **top 10 skills the World Economic Forum projected for 2030** and how they relate to leadership beyond gender norms.

These skills include creative thinking, analytical thinking, technological literacy, curiosity, resilience, flexibility, agility, system thinking, AI and data literacy, motivation, self-awareness, talent management, and service orientation.

Let's look deeper into how these ten skills will benefit you as a leader breaking out of the traditional gender roles.

1. **Creative Thinking:** As leaders beyond gender norms, we must creatively challenge and reshape traditional paradigms, fostering innovation in diversity and inclusion initiatives.

2. **Analytical Thinking:** The responsibility lies in dissecting deeply ingrained biases and making informed decisions that promote gender equity, ensuring a fair and balanced workplace.

3. **Technological Literacy:** Embracing digital literacy is crucial for dismantling gender barriers in tech industries and ensuring equal opportunities.

4. **Curiosity and Lifelong Learning:** Curiosity fuels our journey, pushing us to continuously explore new perspectives and dismantle stereotypes. A leader's responsibility is to inspire this thirst for knowledge in their teams.

5. **Resilience, Flexibility, and Agility:** Adapting to adversity and uncertainties is vital, but as leaders, we must create environments where everyone can thrive regardless of gender.

6. **System Thinking:** Understanding the interconnectedness of diversity and inclusion allows us to address underlying biases and create truly inclusive workplaces.

7. **AI and Data Literacy:** Harnessing AI and data is about efficiency and ensuring our decisions are free from bias, promoting fairness in leadership.

8. **Motivation and Self-awareness:** Leaders should lead by example, showing how self-awareness can lead to the growth of individuals and organisations beyond gender stereotypes.

9. **Talent Management:** Our responsibility is to nurture diverse talent and build collaborative environments where everyone has a chance to shine, irrespective of gender.

10. **Service Orientation and Customer Excellence:** As leaders, we must exemplify exceptional service by ensuring our workplaces prioritise gender equality, thus driving innovation and loyalty.

Section 4: Integrating AI into Leadership

Now, let's dive into the practical integration of AI, such as ChatGPT, into leadership development. AI can be a valuable tool in breaking down gender norms in leadership.

Remember, AI is not without biases, so asking the right questions is crucial for accurate answers.

Here are ten ideas for questions you can ask ChatGPT to help you create a personalised leadership development plan tailored to your strengths and weaknesses, focusing on leadership beyond gender norms.

ChatGPT Prompts to Generate Personalised Leadership Development Plans:

1. "Help me create a leadership development plan tailored to my strengths and weaknesses, becoming a leader who leads beyond gender."

2. "I want to become a leader who leads beyond genders. Can you provide me with a step-by-step plan?"

3. "What key leadership competencies should I focus on for my career growth?"

4. "Please assist me in outlining a leadership development plan that aligns with my long-term career goals."

5. "I want to improve my communication skills as a leader who leads beyond gender. Can you suggest a development plan for me?"

6. "Create a personalised leadership development road map as a leader who leads beyond gender based on my current leadership style."

7. "What critical leadership skills should I prioritise in my development plan?"

8. "Help me design a leadership development plan emphasising emotional intelligence and empathy."

9. "I aim to be a more resilient leader. What steps should I include in my development plan?"

10. "Can you provide a leadership development plan that focuses on fostering diversity and inclusion in my team?"

Additionally, AI can analyse your communication, ensuring your words are inclusive. By understanding and respecting different energy blends, AI can help you communicate more effectively with your team members.

Communications and ChatGPT: My favourite way of using ChatGPT is to communicate with people from their point of view. Understanding where they are coming from, rather than forcing them to believe in me and where I'm coming from, is a transformational experience.

Communicating with People by Understanding Their Blend of Energies

Imagine you can reach out to another person by understanding how they see the world. Or at least you are more aware of their perspective. Can you imagine the difference rather than making assumptions about that person? You can also turn it around. Imagine conversing with someone and that person listens to you to understand, not to be understood.

What if I told you that you can use a free tool such as ChatGPT to do so?

Remember in chapter 6 where I told you about the Vitality Test and how you can find out what your windows to the world look like from the energy perspective?

I'm a massive fan of this test and use it as much as possible with my clients and family and friends.

ChatGPT is a fabulous help in doing so. However, as said before, you need to prepare the chatbot properly. You've got to feed the chatbot with the right ingredients before you ask the bot to analyse a person for you.

Preparing ChatGPT for Future Conversations in a Thread about People's Energy Blends

I start by giving ChatGPT information about the five energies and what they stand for. At the end of that share, I simply say, "At this point, I want you to confirm you have received this information and that you will be using this in the conversations that follow on this thread."

ChatGPT reply:

Thank you for sharing this information about the Chinese Energy field and its five energy characteristics: water, wood, fire, earth, and metal, each with its corresponding soul question. I have received and noted this information, and I'll keep it in mind for future conversations on this thread. Understanding these energy characteristics and their associated soul questions can provide valuable insights into how individuals perceive and interact with the world around them. Feel free to elaborate or ask questions related to this topic, and I'll be happy to engage in discussions based on this knowledge.

From this point, I can ask ChatGPT to analyse people's profiles or advise me on how to reach them for maximum results.

I had one person's profile in front of me, and I felt I didn't understand where he was coming from regarding leadership and gender roles.

Prompt to ChatGPT:

"What three things must I remember when communicating leadership beyond gender with this individual? Water: 29.7% Wood: 18.9% Fire: 13.5% Earth: 10.8% Metal: 27%"

ChatGPT reply:

When communicating with an individual with the energy blend you mentioned (Water: 29.7%, Wood: 18.9%, Fire: 13.5%, Earth: 10.8%, Metal: 27%), it's essential to be mindful of their unique characteristics and preferences.

Here are three key things to remember:

1. ***Emphasise Safety and Clarity***
   a. *Given the individual's relatively high water energy (29.7 percent), they likely value emotional safety and stability. When discussing sensitive topics like gender, prioritise creating a safe and non-judgemental environment.*
   b. *Use clear and straightforward language to convey your points. Avoid ambiguity or uncertainty, which may trigger their tendency to seek reassurance and clarity.*
2. ***Appeal to Growth and Purpose***
   a. *With a significant amount of metal (27 percent) and wood (18.9 percent) energies, this person may be receptive to discussions emphasising personal growth, ambition, and purpose.*
   b. *When discussing changes in the gender space, frame the conversation in a way that highlights how embracing these changes can lead to personal development and contribute positively to society.*
3. ***Respect Their Need for Structure and Order***
   a. *Individuals with solid metal energy (27 percent) often appreciate well-structured and organised information and systems.*
   b. *Provide well-researched and logically presented arguments or information when discussing gender-related topics. Avoid chaotic or emotionally charged discussions that may deter them from engaging in the conversation.*

In addition to these three key considerations, remember to approach the conversation with empathy and open-mindedness. While the person's energy blend can provide insights, it doesn't fully define their beliefs or attitudes.

Be willing to listen actively, ask questions to understand their perspective, and find common ground when possible.

Building a respectful and understanding dialogue can help facilitate productive conversations on complex issues like changes in the gender space.

(All of the advice above comes from ChatGPT.)

I then asked ChatGPT, "What are the three things I should avoid doing when communicating with this individual?"

ChatGPT reply:

When communicating with an individual with the energy blend you've described (Water: 29.7%, Wood: 18.9%, Fire: 13.5%, Earth: 10.8%, Metal: 27%), it's essential to be aware of potential pitfalls that could hinder effective communication.

Here are three things to avoid:

1. ***Avoid Confrontation and Aggressiveness***
   a. *Individuals with higher water and metal energies (Water: 29.7 percent, Metal: 27 percent) may be sensitive and value emotional safety and order. Avoid confrontational or aggressive communication styles that can create discomfort and resistance.*
   b. *Instead, maintain a calm and respectful tone in your discussions, focusing on understanding their perspective rather than attacking their beliefs.*

2. ***Don't Oversimplify or Disregard Their Concerns***

    a. *It's crucial not to oversimplify complex issues related to gender or dismiss their concerns. Their unique experiences and values influence each person's viewpoint.*

    b. *Avoid sweeping generalisations or assuming that their resistance to change is solely due to their energy composition. Take the time to listen to their specific concerns and engage in nuanced discussions.*

3. ***Steer Clear of Emotional Overload***

    a. *Fire energy (13.5 percent) can be associated with passion and emotional expression, but overwhelming emotional intensity in discussions may be ineffective.*

    b. *Avoid emotional overload or making the conversation too emotionally charged, as this can hinder their ability to engage in a rational and thoughtful discussion. Instead, aim for a balanced and constructive exchange of ideas.*

The goal is to foster a respectful and open dialogue that acknowledges their unique energy blend and perspectives while promoting understanding and empathy. By avoiding these communication pitfalls, you can increase the likelihood of productive conversations on sensitive topics like changes in the gender space.

So, my friend, AI can help us on this journey to become better at communicating, bolder at understanding what you haven't understood before, and brighter as a leading light, becoming the change you want to see in your world.

Section 5: The Wisdom of Wendy Watkins

This section will draw inspiration from Wendy Watkins, a dear friend, one of my change makers, a mindset magician, author, mind-body-spirit coach, and laughter luminary. She emphasises that leadership is changing, challenging traditional gender labels. Wendy's wisdom underscores the importance of embracing joy and authenticity in leadership.

Her insights include the significance of aligning actions with personal values, seeking support from mentors, and incorporating humour into leadership.

Shifting Perspectives to Let in More Joy and High Vibrations into Your Life

In one of *The Change Makers Podcast* interview I did with Wendy, she painted a picture of how growth and adaptation are the heartbeats of lifelong learners and leaders beyond gender boundaries. She highlighted the magic of laughter in facing life's challenges and encouraged letting go of negativity, like allowing a cloud to drift away.

In an earlier podcast interview—"Can you be a joyful leader?"—Wendy boldly questioned traditional gender labels in modern leadership. She sparked a conversation about being true to ourselves with joy and authenticity.

In her enlightening talk, Wendy emphasised that leadership is changing. The rigid rules of traditional gender roles are fading, making space for a more genuine and diverse expression of leadership. She highlighted the importance of leaders in creating an environment that values uniqueness over societal norms.

As we journey in leadership beyond gender, the struggle to make space for joy and flow becomes apparent.

Internal challenges arise from the boxes where we've placed ourselves and others:

- What if "joy" isn't seen as professional in your world?

- What if you're seen as less severe if you embrace joy?

Yet, as you read this, you may yearn to bring more joy and flow into your personal and professional life. These challenges are intense because society clings to stereotypes and fixed ideas. Remember my client story in chapter 6? The CFO who blindly thought he could not show humour at work. Like all of us, he wasn't aware of his subconscious programs and the box he was in.

You might worry if your family or friends will understand your choices if you step outside the lines. You might fear how colleagues will react if you show your true self in your work life.

Remember, these boxes exist only in our minds!

The rewards of breaking free from these challenges are priceless. When leaders embrace joy and flow, they become role models for those around them.

This might mean choosing a path to your passion and inspiring others to do the same. At work, it could lead to a culture that celebrates authenticity, motivating others to embrace their strengths.

Section 6: Embracing Joy and Authenticity

Embracing joy and authenticity in leadership can be challenging due to societal stereotypes. This section will explore the internal challenges when leaders seek to bring more joy and authenticity into their lives and workplaces.

These challenges include concerns about professionalism, fears of being perceived as less severe, and worries about how colleagues, family, and friends will react. However, it's essential to remember that these boxes exist only in our minds.

Integrating joy and flow into leadership has profound benefits. By shedding conventions, leaders can unlock their team's limitless potential. Imagine a workplace where strengths shine and collaboration flourishes because rigid expectations are set aside.

This transformative approach to leadership, where joy accompanies results, creates a resilient and harmonious work atmosphere.

Wendy's wisdom inspired me as a guiding compass through uncharted territory. Her call to honour each team member's essence resonates deeply with those embracing leadership beyond gender.

Section 7: The Rewards of Authentic Leadership

The rewards of embracing joy and authenticity in leadership are profound. This section will delve into the benefits of breaking free from societal expectations and fostering an environment where genuineness thrives.

These rewards include personal growth, collaboration, and creating a resilient and harmonious work atmosphere. Authentic leaders become role models, motivating others to embrace their strengths and unique qualities.

As leaders, our goal is to create an environment where authenticity flourishes. By embracing joy and flow, we pave the way for personal growth and balanced, fulfilling lives for ourselves and our teams.

Wendy's wisdom on joy and leadership is significant. Being an authentic leader means aligning actions with personal values. Wendy encourages us to reflect on moments when we aren't true to our values, spurring continuous growth.

Seeking support from coaches, friends, or mentors helps us define our values, acting as a compass on our leadership journey. **And the role of humour in leadership! Wendy showed that humour adds colour to authentic leadership.**

In a world often filled with seriousness, Wendy invites us to embrace laughter on our leadership journey. So, fellow explorers, let's embrace the joy of lifelong learning, transforming into beacons of change.

As Wendy Watkins said, "The future of leadership lies in those who embrace gender fluidity and genuine self-expression."

Can you hear the call to join this transformative evolution?

Section 8: The Future of Leadership

In this final section, we'll emphasise the future of leadership, which lies in embracing gender fluidity and genuine self-expression. The call to join this transformative evolution is evident.

The chapter concludes by encouraging readers to hear this call and become part of the change, leading with authenticity, joy, and an open mind in a world that values uniqueness over societal norms.

In closing, let's heed the call of this transformative evolution.

Here's how we can move forward:

> **Step 1: Embrace Lifelong Learning**—Make curiosity your ally. Explore new perspectives and welcome change as an opportunity for growth.

Step 2: Foster Authenticity—Break free from societal boxes. Embrace joy and flow, setting an example that resonates with those around you.

Step 3: Lead with Laughter—Infuse humour into your leadership style.

Use it as a powerful tool to navigate challenges with a light heart.

Together, we can be leaders who thrive in an ever-changing world, igniting a symphony of authenticity, growth, and joy that resonates far beyond the confines of gender.

To close this long and important chapter, moving forward, three crucial steps are:

1. **Embrace Authenticity and Curiosity**: Leaders prioritise self-awareness, self-leadership, self-love, and humour. Be authentic in your actions and curious about the world around you. Challenge traditional gender norms and biases by creating an environment where everyone can thrive, irrespective of gender.

2. **Lifelong Learning**: Continuously develop the skills projected for the future by organisations like the World Economic Forum. These skills include creative thinking, analytical thinking, technological literacy, curiosity, resilience, and more. Commit to being a leader who fosters growth and learning in your team.

3. **Integrate AI Thoughtfully**: Utilise AI, such as ChatGPT, as a tool for leadership development as you aspire to lead people without the boxes your unconscious mind has placed them into. Ask AI-driven questions to create personalised development plans, and leverage AI's communication analysis to ensure inclusivity. However, remain mindful of AI biases and always ask the right questions for accurate insights.

In conclusion, the future of leadership lies in embracing authenticity, curiosity, and AI integration while challenging traditional gender norms.

By taking these crucial steps, you can become a beacon of change and lead with joy, openness, and authenticity in a world that values uniqueness over societal norms.

<h1 style="text-align:center">CHAPTER 19</h1>

<h1 style="text-align:center">Leaving a Legacy:
Lighting the Path for Future Leaders</h1>

As we strive towards the culmination of our remarkable journey, it's time to cast our gaze beyond the horizon and ponder the legacy that will mark our passage through this world.

In this pivotal chapter, we shall delve into the realm of impact, reflecting on the indelible mark we can make and charting a course to ensure that our influence resonates through the annals of time. So, let's embark on this final odyssey, my friend, and ignite a trail that will guide future leaders regardless of gender, transcending the barriers that once confined us.

Think about it. Becoming known and remembered as an inspirational leader is like painting the sky with vibrant hues. It's a testament to your unwavering dedication, ability to challenge conventions, and commitment to sparking change. Being an inspirational leader isn't just about leaving footprints on the sands of time; it's about creating a lasting masterpiece that inspires future generations.

Consider the boundless benefits that await those who dare to carve their path as inspirational leaders. You become a beacon of hope, a torchbearer whose light dispels darkness and ignites passion. You wield power to transform not only your life but also the lives of those who cross your path. Your legacy reverberates through the corridors of history, a melody of empowerment and change.

Yet, let's not ignore the constant challenges that pepper our journey.

Ah, yeah, challenges—those often-misunderstood companions that, when embraced, morph into opportunities. These hurdles test our mettle, pushing us beyond our comfort zones and demanding our utmost resilience.

As we stand at the precipice of gender-defying leadership, these challenges cease to be stumbling blocks. They metamorphose into stepping-stones propelling us towards greatness. These challenges are our opportunities. These challenges are the cornerstone of our internal expansion to guide ourselves and others from a place of authenticity, freedom, and value. Turning these challenges into opportunities will give you profound insights into the diversity of humanity.

Uncovering Wisdom That Defies Norms and Ignites Change

As I embarked on the journey writing this book, I aimed to uncover the wisdom that defies norms and ignites change.

In doing so, I also embarked on over 150 podcast interviews for *The Change Makers Podcast*. I've mentioned some of them already in this book.

In this chapter, I will drill deeper into Mahmud Samandari's divine wisdom. Mahmud is a true visionary in the realm of leadership that transcends the limitations of gender. In our candid conversation in the podcast episode #154 on "Trust: A Catalyst for Change," Mahmud shared his transformative perspective on what leadership truly means.

Mahmud said: "Leadership is not about one person at the helm; it's about nurturing ideas, steering collectives, and inspiring organisations to flourish."

His insight is refreshingly straightforward yet profoundly impactful: *Leadership should be an all-encompassing force that values the contributions of every individual.*

I agree with Mahmud and wholeheartedly believe in the power of universal participation, where everyone's unique abilities, experiences, and instincts are brought into the fold.

As I've repeatedly said in this book, nobody says doing so is easy. However, the effect it can make your organisation is so breathtakingly unique and desirable that you will see the internal and external rewards. In other words, priceless outcomes!

In Mahmud's world, leadership is a tapestry woven with competence, innovation, and collaboration—a realm where the constraints of gender are left behind. In our conversation, Mahmud emphasised a crucial facet of leadership—the legacy we leave behind.

"Tell me who you surround yourself with, and I'll tell you who you are!"

Now, let's dive into something many shy away from: the profound impact of the people we surround ourselves with.

You've probably heard it a million times, but it bears repeating: We are, in many ways, a reflection of the five people we spend the most time with.

Take a moment to let that sink in.

If your inner circle consists of individuals who conform to societal norms without question, you might soon find yourself on the same well-trodden path, marching to the beat of mediocrity. Conversely, if you're rubbing shoulders with visionaries, trailblazers, and dreamers, their energy can ignite your ambitions, propelling you closer to your goals.

Remember, your circle isn't just a reflection of who you are; it also shapes how you perceive yourself and how the world perceives you. Think of it as a mirror that reflects your potential back at you. Surrounding yourself with those who challenge, inspire, and elevate your perspective can be a game-changer. When you're backed by a tribe that believes in your ability to lead beyond gender, the walls of doubt and insecurity crumble.

Let me illustrate this with a couple of examples to underscore the importance of your circle in your journey towards becoming a leader who transcends gender norms.

Example 1: Imagine your inner circle comprises individuals with staunchly traditional views on gender roles. They frequently discuss how men and women should behave and their societal roles. Over time, these conversations become a constant presence in your life, and gradually, these assumptions seep into your consciousness. As you witness your friends conforming to these stereotypes, your brain begins to accept these roles as the norm. Subconsciously, you internalise these assumptions as truths, solidifying your belief in their permanence.

Example 2: Now, picture a different scenario. Your closest friends are forward-thinking individuals who actively challenge traditional gender norms. They recognise that they can hold space for a number of different ideas and things at the same time, focus on who they are, and not be afraid to give people the opportunity to share their perspectives. These people celebrate diversity, embrace fluidity, and engage in conversations that question established roles. In this environment, your assumptions are continually challenged and reshaped. As you witness your friends break free from societal constraints and passionately pursue their goals regardless of gender, your own beliefs expand. You start to internalise that individuals aren't limited to predefined roles but have the power to forge their own paths. Exposure to diverse perspectives erodes the foundation of traditional stereotypes, making space for new, inclusive beliefs to take root.

Now, let's talk about the power and challenge of social media algorithms. In today's digital age, social media and algorithms play a significant role in shaping our worldview. If your online interactions mirror your offline circle—dominated by conventional thinkers—the content, you consume will reinforce existing stereotypes. Algorithms track your preferences and serve content that aligns with your beliefs, creating an echo chamber that further cements those notions. This is where the danger lies. Your feed becomes an endless loop of content that reinforces your assumptions, creating the illusion that these beliefs are universally accepted.

And what happens in the comfort zone of these "norms"?

Let's say you're part of a group of friends who never challenge traditional norms. You all share posts, memes, and articles perpetuating conventional gender roles. Women are pigeonholed into one category, men into another. Your feed becomes saturated with these perspectives, and the content you encounter affirms what you've always known.

The outcome? As you scroll through your social media feeds, your beliefs become more robust, making you less likely to question the status quo.

But on the flip side, imagine you're part of a circle of visionaries and change-makers—leaders who transcend traditional gender norms. In this group, you all share articles about breaking stereotypes, promoting equality, and challenging standards. Your feed becomes a wellspring of diverse perspectives, constantly pushing the boundaries of your assumptions. You're exposed to stories of individuals smashing through barriers, shattering expectations, and reshaping the narrative.

As you engage with this content, your beliefs start to evolve. You begin to see that the world is vast, complex, and full of possibilities beyond traditional gender roles.

So, who do you aspire to become?

In the realm of energies, within ourselves and our interactions with the world, lies the essence of transformation. Every thought, every feeling, and every action first originate in the field of energies—the intricate interplay of our minds and hearts. It's a continuous process, often unnoticed, yet it moulds the person and leader we can become.

The company we keep, both in person and online, profoundly influences our assumptions and beliefs about gender roles. When we surround ourselves with those who challenge traditional norms, we embark on a journey of profound change. Conversely, if we remain ensconced within our comfort zones, we inadvertently perpetuate stagnant ideologies. The power to shift this narrative rests within our choices—who we want to be.

Diversifying our circles to include diverse perspectives, curating the content we consume, and actively seeking viewpoints that broaden our horizons can be transformative. Moreover, understanding the science of quantum physics and epigenetics opens a gateway to our fullest potential. Dr. Joe Dispenza's pioneering work and research in meditation illuminate how we can harness this understanding to effect significant changes in our lives.

By delving into the depths of our energies through meditation, we can access a profound understanding of ourselves. This process aligns seamlessly with the principles of quantum physics and epigenetics, showcasing our immense capacity to transform ourselves and the world.

Having practised meditation daily for over a decade, I can attest to its profound impact on one's well-being, awareness, and perspective on the world.

Ultimately, it all begins with knowing ourselves and defining who we aspire to become. With this self-awareness and a deeper comprehension of the science of energies, we hold the key to unlocking transformative change within ourselves and our broader society.

But here's the catch . . .

As you embark on this journey, be prepared to say goodbye to those who no longer align with your vision. As you become an inspirational leader, some chapters must conclude to make way for new beginnings. It's not about turning your back on your past but courageously stepping into a future where your authenticity thrives.

This chapter isn't just about setting intentions for the legacy you wish to leave; it's about actively designing the tapestry of impact. It's about casting your light so brilliantly that it continues to shine even when you're no longer at the forefront. It's about creating a ripple effect that influences generations, a testament to the fact that leadership isn't bound by gender but by the power of the human spirit.

So, as we conclude this transformative voyage, let's ponder:

1. **What kind of impact do you aspire to leave behind?**

   Envision the footprints you want to imprint on the sands of time, the echoes of change you wish to resonate through the ages.

2. **How do you see yourself as a catalyst for future leaders?**

    Consider how your journey can light the way for those who follow a luminous path towards leadership excellence.

3. **Are you ready to surround yourself with the tribe that uplifts your spirit?**

    Reflect on the company you keep. Are they your biggest cheerleaders or subtle detractors? How might a shift in your circle elevate your journey?

As I pen the final chapters of this transformative voyage, remember, my friend, you're not just leaving a legacy—you're igniting a flame that will guide future leaders, transcending genders and soaring towards a world where authentic leadership knows no bounds.

The moment is now, the time is ripe, and the legacy you're about to craft is beyond extraordinary.

CHAPTER 20

Becoming the Torchbearer:
Embracing Your Leadership Beyond Gender

Embrace the quantum leap in leadership,
where the future belongs to those
who think beyond their boxes,
harness the power of technology
and lead with the light of authenticity and diversity.

As we embark on this final chapter of our journey through *Beyond Gender: The New Rules of Leadership*, we must reflect on the transformative voyage we've taken together.

We've shattered the gender matrix, defied peer pressure from the past, unearthed our superpowers, and blurred the lines of masculinity and femininity. After all, as we've looked at it, just labelling traits as feminine or masculine is not setting us free from the social construct; it is reinforcing stereotyping. We've liberated our language, found joy in leadership, gracefully navigated obstacles, and harnessed the power of allies.

Vulnerability has become our strength, and we've challenged the status quo, unmasking the intricate dance of gender identity and roles. We've created ripples of change, ignited innovation, and redefined success.

We've fostered a culture of belonging, empowered the next generation, upheld integrity, embraced lifelong learning, and left the groundwork for future leaders.

Let's look ahead to the future we're about to shape.

This chapter stands on the precipice of a new era, the Fifth Industrial Revolution. And to explain, the Fifth Industrial Revolution merges human-centric values with advanced technological and biological systems to foster inclusive, sustainable growth and enhance individual empowerment. A time when leadership isn't just about following the old rules; it's about rewriting them. The leaders of tomorrow are willing to unlearn, adapt, and, most importantly, think beyond their boxes. It's a quantum leap in leadership, where we hold multiple perspectives simultaneously.

The first step in this journey is recognising to our core that our conditioning, our beliefs about gender, and the limitations society has imposed upon us are not THE TRUTH, the WHOLE truth, and nothing but the truth. They are constructs shaped by history and culture—and only that. Let's not give these constructs too much food to chew on. Let's focus more on setting ourselves and others free to become the highest versions of ourselves.

We must become deeply aware of this conditioning to be the architects of leadership beyond gender.

We must be courageous enough to question, deconstruct, and rebuild our understanding of leadership.

As we head into the Fifth Industrial Revolution, the fusion of technology and human potential is our greatest asset. Quantum computers and AI can be our partners in creating a better world, **but we must do our bit for it to be successful for all.**

AI can handle complex tasks, freeing our minds to focus on creativity, innovation, and ethical decision-making. But to harness this power, we must become quantum humans who can simultaneously hold more than two things in their minds.

We must give space in our hearts and minds for our new identity and rewrite our stories to empower us to live in harmony with ourselves and technology.

We must be able to imagine a world where leaders are not bound by binary thinking but can navigate the intricate dance of multiple perspectives. Once we can imagine it, we can create it!

It's a world where we embrace diversity not as a checkbox but as the essence of our leadership. It's a world where leadership transcends gender, and we celebrate everyone's unique qualities, skills, and talents.

As pioneers of this new era, we must lead by example. We must be willing to challenge the norms, disrupt the status quo, and inspire change. Enabling us to do so, we must find joy in the process, even in adversity, and lead with unwavering integrity. We must keep reminding ourselves that life is happening for us, not to us!

The path ahead will be challenging. We will encounter resistance, but we must remember that every revolution faces pushback. We can persevere, stand united, and embrace the vulnerability that will make a difference. We are the leaders who will create a culture of belonging where everyone is seen, valued, and respected.

Mentorship becomes our gift to the next generation. We pass on knowledge and the courage to be different and unleash and embrace our creativity. We model critical thinking, the wisdom to challenge norms, and the resilience to face setbacks. Together, we build a legacy that lights the path for future leaders.

In conclusion, dear readers, as we enter the Fifth Industrial Revolution, let us become the torchbearers of leadership beyond gender. Let us embrace our roles as quantum humans, unafraid of complexity and capable of holding multiple truths.

Let us use technology and AI to amplify our potential and create a better world. And let us remember that leadership is not defined by gender but by our ability to inspire, innovate, and lead with integrity.

The future is ours to shape, and together, we will illuminate the path for future generations.

Thank you for joining me on this extraordinary journey.

Reykjavík, Iceland, October 22, 2023

Rúna Magnúsdóttir

ACKNOWLEDGEMENTS

Behind every great book, an even greater bunch of people are rolling their eyes at my out-of-the-box antics. They stuck around, so here's my chance to say a massive *takk* (thanks in Icelandic)!

First, a massive shout-out to the brainy and brilliant Dr David Paul and the ever-insightful Nicholas 'Nick Haines; these two are like the Sherlock and Watson of neuroscience, energy waves and mindfulness, digging deep into the enigmas of humanity with a shovel made of wisdom and a spade of experience. Their support, time, and resources have been as boundless as the potential of the human spirit we often chatted about. They've been with me through thick and thin in the No More Boxes Transformational Movement.

Then there's the Change-Makers squad – Gido, Monique, Susanne, Bev, Wendy and Nick – who's been with me every step. I couldn't have stirred the pot of traditional gender roles without your insights and wisdom.

Now, for the unsung heroes: every soul who's supported me emotionally, financially, or by simply nodding to my rants about societal conditioning. You're the backbone of this endeavour, and your belief in this project has been the wind beneath my somewhat unconventional wings.

A special thanks to my dear friend, Bjarney Lúðvíksdóttir, for her unique friendship and endless support.

Last but not least, my family: my rock and better half, Óli, who's endured my 'creative' phases with the patience of a saint, and my kids, Magnús Ingi and Birgitta Rún, you've been my grounding force, reality check, and biggest cheerleader, even when my ideas seemed to come from a galaxy far away.

In conclusion, if this book makes waves, it's because of all of you.

If it doesn't, well, we had a blast trying, didn't we?

Here's to breaking boxes and building bridges.

Skál!

Rúna

ABOUT THE AUTHOR:
RÚNA MAGNÚSDÓTTIR

Rúna Magnúsdóttir, a.k.a. Rúna Magnús, a leading authority in crafting tomorrow's leadership, is a visionary and change maker.

Born, raised, and thriving in Iceland, Runa has been a lifetime entrepreneur, first diving into the business world with her mother's wholesale company, Bergís, and later transforming her career into a beacon of personal leadership and empowerment.

Renowned for her talks, coaching and mentoring, Rúna has worked with organisations like the Enterprising Europe in Malta, Kaos Pilot in Denmark and Madison University, Wisconsin, among others.

Her speaking engagements span prestigious events and locations such as INBOUND in Boston, Elevate in Oslo, NAWBO National Conferences in the USA, JUMP in Paris, and The Network for Transformational Leaders in the UK.

She has been featured in media outlets, including the Huffington Post, Forbes, Phycology, Breathe, The Times and Finnair Magazine.

Rúna's achievements have been recognised with numerous awards, including being named one of the 15 Visionary Leaders Shaping the Leadership World in 2023 by US Reporter, receiving the Woman Economic Forum Awards in 2022, and the Leadership of the Year Award from The Network for Transformational Leaders in 2019.

Her journey as an author began with impactful titles like her personal branding book 'Branding Your X-Factor' and co-authored 'The Story Of Boxes, The Good, The Bad and The Ugly'. Her latest venture, 'Beyond Gender: The New Rules of Leadership', is a manifesto for future leaders, challenging traditional gender roles and societal norms with out-of-the-box ideas and strategies.

REFERENCE GUIDE

Source Last Name	Source First Name	Source Title	Publication Year	Type of Course	Publisher Name
Frandsen	Susanne	"Breaking Free from the Box: Leading Through Change and Innovation for Success"	2023	*The Change Makers Podcast #145*	The Change Makers Podcast
Grossman	Leslie	"How Leaders Build Their Entourage"	2017	*The Change Makers Podcast #5*	The Change Makers Podcast
Haines	Nicholas	"Why Men Are NOT from Mars, and Women Are NOT from Venus"	2020	*The Change Makers Podcast #128*	The Change Makers Podcast
Hancock	Bev	"Changing the World a One Conversation at the Time"	2023	*The Change Makers Podcast #150*	The Change Makers Podcast
Paul	Dr David	"Breaking Free from Gender Conditioning with Mindfulness"	2023	*The Change Makers Podcast #149*	The Change Makers Podcast
Rippon	Gina	"The Gendered Brain"	2020	*The Change Makers Podcast #116*	The Change Makers Podcast
Rippon	Gina	*The Gendered Brain - The New Neuroscience That Shatters the Myth of the Female Brain*	2019	Book	Bodley Head
Thorhallsdottir	Thordis Loa	"The Hidden Problem: Addressing Gender Imbalance and Biases in Icelandic Leadership"	23	*The Change Makers Podcast #147*	The Change Makers Podcast

Samandari	Mahmud	"Trust: A Catalyst for Change with Mahmud Samandari"	2023	*The Change Makers Podcast* #154	The Change Makers Podcast
Schimanski	Gido	"The Ripple Effect: Changing Inner Worlds, Transforming the Environment"	2023	*The Change Makers Podcast* #146	The Change Makers Podcast
Singh	Neerja	"Breaking Barriers: Bridging Generational Divides for Leadership Beyond Gender"	2023	*The Change Makers Podcast* #148	The Change Makers Podcast
Watkins	Wendy	"The Power of Laughter in Leadership: Embracing Growth and Authenticity"	2023	*The Change Makers Podcast* #152	The Change Makers Podcast
Whitmore	Sir John	Coaching for Performance	1992	Leadership Coaching	https://www.performanceconsultants.com/coaching-for-performance-book
		Gallup Survey on the Third Shift	2023	Gallup Polls	https://www.ruv.is/frettir/innlent/2023-10-01-verkaskipting-a-islenskum-heimilum-ojofn-og-kynjud-392821
		World Economic Forum - Future Skills	2023	Future of Work Skills 2025 by WEF	https://www.weforum.org/agenda/2023/05/future-of-jobs-2023-skills/
		Hewlett Packard Diversity Plan	2021	Hewlett Packard Diversity Plan 2030	https://press.hp.com/us/en/press-releases/2021/hp-shares-ambitious-2030-goals-to-drive-DEI-in-tech-industry.html
		OECD Women Economic Empowerment	2021	Research OECD Women Economic Empowerment	https://www.oecd.org/development/gender-development/How-does-aid-support-womens-economic-empowerment-2021.pdf